COMFORT ONE ANOTHER

A DEVOTIONAL STUDY OF 1 & 2 THESSALONIANS

PASTOR RUSTY YOST

WESTBOW
PRESS
A DIVISION OF THOMAS NELSON

WestBow Press books may be ordered through booksellers or by contacting:

WestBow Press
A Division of Thomas Nelson
1663 Liberty Drive
Bloomington, IN 47403
www.westbowpress.com
1-(866) 928-1240

Scripture taken from the King James Version of the Bible.

ISBN: 978-1-4908-0289-3 (sc)
ISBN: 978-1-4908-0291-6 (hc)
ISBN: 978-1-4908-0290-9 (e)

Library of Congress Control Number: 2013913090

Printed in the United States of America.

WestBow Press rev. date: 8/6/2013

DEDICATION

It is a great joy for me to dedicate my first book to my family. Every man owes a debt of gratitude to those around him who love, support, mold, and encourage him to pursue God's will and to live for Christ. I first acknowledge the wonderful influence of three precious ladies God placed in my life—my mother, Shelby Yost, and my two grandmothers, Lilly Yost and Myrtle Hardy. I look forward to meeting them again in heaven.

I would also like to acknowledge the godly influence of my father, Clyde R. Yost Sr. Dad's spiritual influence upon my life began on the day he rededicated his life to Christ. His decision to follow Christ gave me the courage to step forward during the same invitation and receive Christ as my Savior when I was a ten-year-old boy.

I would also like to thank my father-in-law and pastor, Shelby Gillam, for his godly influence upon my life over the years and for his encouragement to begin writing and actually bring a book into existence. By God's grace, this will be the first of other works to follow.

Of course, this dedication would not be complete without acknowledging the most important gift God has placed in my life—my dear wife, Deb. My wife is a true helpmeet who blesses my life in many ways each day. I appreciate her love for me, her children, her grandchildren, and all of her family. Without her love for Christ and partnership in ministry, my life simply would not be what it is today.

To all of my immediate and extended family, I say thank you. I love each of you, and may the God of all comfort be your abiding strength until we meet at last in his presence.

TABLE OF CONTENTS

Introduction ix

1 Thessalonians 1 1

1 Thessalonians 2 11

1 Thessalonians 3 23

1 Thessalonians 4 31

1 Thessalonians 5 47

2 Thessalonians 1 63

2 Thessalonians 2 77

2 Thessalonians 3 99

Comfort One Another 109

For more information on the ministry of
Pastor Yost visit the websites below:

cbmtoday.org

or

pastorrusty.com

INTRODUCTION

Paul's experience at Thessalonica began when he boldly shared the gospel with a people steeped in idolatry and immorality. Immediately upon hearing the gospel, a powerful work occurred in their hearts, resulting in an amazing transformation of their lives. This wonderful work of the Spirit in the lives of a people so lost in spiritual darkness should serve as a source of inspiration in our own day. Thankfully, *no one* is beyond the reach of the gospel, including the many in our beloved nation who seem so far from God.

The apostle Paul's letters to the young church at Thessalonica are filled with practical application for our lives today. If you are hungry for spiritual growth, this devotional study is for you! I have no doubt the Holy Spirit will enrich your walk with Christ as you engage in this verse-by-verse study.

Your journey through these two letters will also introduce you to the great doctrine of the second coming of Jesus Christ. In his first letter, Paul's answer to a question posed by this young church subsequently brought comfort to the hearts of every succeeding generation of believers, including our own! In his second letter, the apostle continued to clarify various details concerning the second coming that are simply fascinating. There are several mountain peaks of Bible prophecy to be discovered in this study, and I'm sure you will find it quite exciting.

I hope you will take the time to make full use of the suggested activities that appear throughout the text of this book. These activities will promote additional Scripture reading and the use of other outside resources to enhance your study. As well, the questions presented will compel you to think more deeply about the text we are studying. The various questions can also be useful for group study.

At the end of the book, I have included an addendum designed to comfort and encourage those working through grief associated with the loss of someone dear in life. In my view, the theme verse of Paul's letters to the Thessalonians can be found in the first epistle in 4:18, which says, "Wherefore comfort one another with these words." The promise of Christ's return is to be a constant source of comfort to our hearts as we face inevitable seasons of loss in our lives. I believe the addendum will be a helpful resource that complements this central teaching of Paul to the Thessalonians.

I pray the Lord will prosper your time in his Word as you enjoy this study.

Pastor Rusty Yost

CHAPTER 1

1 THESSALONIANS 1

1 Thessalonians 1:1

> Paul, and Silvanus, and Timotheus, unto the church of the Thessalonians which is in God the Father and in the Lord Jesus Christ: Grace be unto you, and peace, from God our Father, and the Lord Jesus Christ. (1 Thess. 1:1)

The apostle Paul wrote to the church of Thessalonica not long after his initial visit resulted in the formation of a new church. He opens this letter by acknowledging two men who ministered with him during his stay at Thessalonica. Silvanus (Silas) and Timotheus (Timothy) were dependable coworkers who traveled extensively with the apostle during his missionary activities.

Suggested Activities

Using an appropriate map in your Bible or another resource, locate the city of Thessalonica.

Using a Bible dictionary, take the time to read some background information on the city of Thessalonica.

Read the following Bible passage concerning Paul's coworker Silas: Acts 15:22-41.

Read the following Bible passages concerning Paul's coworker Timothy: Acts 16:1–5; 1 Corinthians 4:17; 1 Timothy 1:1–2.

Read Acts 17:1–14 concerning Paul's first visit to Thessalonica.

Please note that Paul wrote to the ***church*** at Thessalonica. The local church is not a manmade idea. Rather, it is the Holy Spirit who speaks of the assembly of believers in a local body. Every able-bodied, born-again believer should be active in a local New Testament church with a pastor(s), deacons, and the fellow saints. Please read 1 Timothy 3 for additional study.

You will note the reference to the Lord Jesus Christ in this opening verse. Paul uses this title nineteen times in his two epistles to the Thessalonians! It should be pointed out that *all* true Christians acknowledge Jesus as Lord. Furthermore, this title is indicative of his deity (cf. Phil. 2:9–11). The word *Lord* is equivalent to the Old Testament word *Jehovah*. As the apostle Peter declared on the day of Pentecost, "Therefore let all the house of Israel know assuredly, that God hath made that same Jesus, whom ye crucified, both Lord and Christ" (Acts 2:36). The Lord Jesus Christ is the unique Son of the living God. He is God come in the person of Jesus, the Christ (John 1:1, 14). As such, he is Lord over all. It is absolutely essential that one come to grips with the fact that Jesus Christ is Lord. Otherwise, one will be lost!

1 Thessalonians 1:2–10

We give thanks to God always for you all, making mention of you in our prayers; remembering without ceasing your work of faith, and labour of love, and patience of hope in our Lord Jesus Christ, in the sight of God and our Father; knowing, brethren beloved, your election of God. For our gospel came not unto you in word only, but also in power, and in the Holy Ghost, and in much assurance; as ye know what manner of men we were among you for your sake. And ye became followers of us, and of the Lord, having received the word in much affliction, with joy of the Holy Ghost: so that ye were ensamples to all that believe in Macedonia and Achaia. For from you sounded out the word of the Lord not only in Macedonia and Achaia, but also in every place your faith to God-ward is spread abroad; so that we need not to speak any thing. For they themselves shew of us what manner of entering in we had unto you, and how ye turned to God from idols to serve the living and true God; and to wait for his Son from heaven, whom he raised from the dead, even Jesus, which delivered us from the wrath to come.

Suggested Activities

In verse 2, Paul speaks of praying for the Thessalonians. Prayer for fellow believers is an important part of our prayer lives. Create a written list with the names of several believers you will pray for regularly. Refresh the list as often as you feel impressed.

List some ways in which you may be able to get involved in the "work of faith" (v. 3) at your local church.

The primary "work of faith" for any church is to reach out actively to those who are lost. Are you concerned about the lost around you? Actively show your concern by developing the habit of inviting others to church and by handing out gospel tracts on a regular basis. Secure a supply of gospel tracts from your church for personal use.

It is interesting to note that *faith, hope,* and *charity* are mentioned in verse 3 (cf. 1 Cor. 13:13). Along with that observation, there are several lessons we should glean from verse 3. First, Paul speaks of their work of faith. This is the only way to do God's work! We must obey God by faith to accomplish anything to his glory. We must trust him to work through us and to supply the needs of the work. Next, Paul speaks of the church's labor of love. Love must always be our motive in ministry. Only believers filled with the love of Christ are properly equipped to carry the gospel to the lost around them. Then Paul speaks of the church's patience of hope. This speaks of the need for persistent witness while waiting for fruit in the lives of those we desire to win to Christ. We must not grow discouraged. Instead, we shall reap if we faint not (Gal. 6:9)!

While serving Christ we must also do so with the blessed hope of his return abiding in our heart (Titus 2:13). Through all of our spiritual battles, we wait patiently for his return. The glorious hope of Christ's return is our sustaining strength in the face of all we may encounter in this life. Child of God, keep looking up! The Lord is coming in great power and glory! He will one day usher us into his presence where all is joy! His reward is with him to give to every man according to his work (Rev. 22:12). Our labor is never in vain in the Lord (1 Cor. 15:58). What a wonderful hope we possess in Christ! Such a glorious hope is the basis for patience as we endure whatever opposition the world may bring against us.

In verse 4, the apostle Paul speaks of the *election* of the believers in Thessalonica. Believers respond to the call of God. It is the blessed Holy Spirit who *initiates* the work of salvation in the hearts of those who believe. His gracious influences bring us to a place of repentance toward God and faith toward our Lord Jesus Christ. Unless the Father draws the sinner through the convicting work of the Holy Spirit, none would ever be saved (cf. John 6:35–44). It is of the greatest importance not to *resist* the Holy Spirit's work in the heart (Acts 7:51). The Thessalonians did not resist the Holy Spirit; rather, they possessed a strong testimony of their election by virtue of turning from idols to serve the living God and his Son, the Lord Jesus Christ.

Suggested Activities

Definition: Election means that sovereign act of God whereby he graciously chose all those he foreknew in Jesus Christ for salvation.

Please read the following passages related to the subject of election: Ephesians 1:3–13; Romans 8:28–38; 1 Peter 1:2.

Question: How is it possible for God to choose a people in eternity past and simultaneously maintain the integrity of man's free will?

Would you agree that it is impossible for a finite creature (man) to fully comprehend the mind of the infinite God?

Point to ponder: It is important for the believer to recognize that the content of God's written revelation is not intended to enable us to probe the depths of God's nature fully. Rather the things written are aimed at producing the full assurance of salvation in the heart of every true believer. With that said, what should you understand about your salvation in light of the fact that you are one of God's elect?

Paul speaks of "knowing" or recognizing the election of these believers. What indication did these people give that they were elected (real believers)? What evidence is there in your own life that you are a true believer?

Point to ponder: *The fact of election can only be known after one is saved.*

In verse 5, Paul reflects upon the powerful work of the gospel in the hearts of the Thessalonians. As laborers for our Lord, we must never lose sight of the inherent power of the gospel message. It is the truth of the gospel that changes lives! Furthermore, we must constantly rely upon the Holy Spirit to work in the hearts of those we desire to win for Christ. The Thessalonians experienced the convicting work of the Spirit, and when they received Christ, the Spirit filled their hearts with *much assurance* concerning their salvation.

The obvious demonstration of the work of the Holy Spirit in the Thessalonians should serve to teach us all that there is no other way to build the church, of which local assemblies are just a part. Human effort can build a beehive of activity, but only the Holy Spirit can build *the* church!

Suggested Activities

Question: How is it that the Thessalonians became followers of Paul and Silas? Isn't it sufficient to say that they simply became followers of the Lord? Why then the reference to following Paul and Silas and Timothy (v. 6)?

How is it possible to have joy and affliction at the same time (v. 6)?

Paul speaks of the example of the Thessalonians in verse 7. In what ways could you follow their example?

Why was it so evident that the Thessalonians were true believers (vv. 9–10).

Point to ponder: To serve the living and true God, one must accept his Son!

What idols are prevalent in our culture today?

Find a definition of the following: humanism, atheism, pantheism, and occultism.

It should be noted that the apostle Paul repeatedly affirmed the bodily resurrection of Jesus from the dead (v. 10). The resurrection of Jesus from the dead is the centerpiece of all the apostolic teaching contained in the New Testament. Likewise, it must be the central part of our preaching today. Of course, it is the bodily resurrection of Jesus from the dead that settles the question of world religions. How is one to muddle through all the confusion as to which religion is true? Well, the resurrection of Jesus answers this question once and for all! His bodily resurrection makes it abundantly clear that he is the way, the truth, and the life, and no man can come to the Father but by him (John 14:6). Thankfully, all those who will confess him as Lord and Savior will be delivered from the wrath of God to come.

CHAPTER 2

1 THESSALONIANS 2

1 Thessalonians 2:1–4

> For yourselves, brethren, know our entrance in unto you, that it was not in vain: but even after that we had suffered before, and were shamefully entreated, as ye know, at Philippi, we were bold in our God to speak unto you the gospel of God with much contention. For our exhortation was not of deceit, nor of uncleanness, nor in guile: but as we were allowed of God to be put in trust with the gospel, even so we speak; not as pleasing men, but God, which trieth our hearts.

Prior to his arrival at Thessalonica, the authorities at Philippi mistreated the apostle Paul. In spite of his citizenship and the right to due process, Paul was beaten and cast into jail without cause. After his release, the apostle continued with his missionary activity and soon arrived in Thessalonica. Instead of a timid approach in light of his recent opposition in Philippi, Paul boldly proclaimed the gospel to the people of Thessalonica. His clear, honest presentation of the gospel entrusted to his care was not in vain. Rather, as the new believers at Thessalonica could now attest, Paul's declaration of the gospel resulted in their radical departure from idolatry to serve the living and true God and his Son, the Lord Jesus Christ.

It is important to note that the gospel message is the gospel of God. Paul was allowed or approved by God to be put in *trust* of the gospel. Paul understood that he was responsible for the proper care of the message of the gospel. Therefore, he had to proclaim that message faithfully to the people in its purity and simplicity. He also had to communicate that message with a pure motive. Failure to minister the gospel with a pure motive could have led to the impression that the gospel message lacked authenticity and was just another means for a charlatan to take advantage of gullible people. The Thessalonians were not only changed by the power of the gospel but were also witnesses who could confirm the sincerity and pure motives with which the apostle served (v. 10).

Paul declared that his exhortation (preaching and teaching) had no element of deceit. Rather, he delivered the gospel in its purity with absolutely no intent to mislead the hearers. Nor did the apostle use a crafty approach aimed at hiding part of the truth from plain view. The apostle understood that he could not minister the gospel with an eye on pleasing men! Since he was entrusted with such a great responsibility before God, he sought only to please God, who tries the heart.

Suggested Activities

Read Acts 16 for the full history behind Paul's reference to the city of Philippi in verse 2.

Read 1 Timothy 1:11–12. What does it mean for the gospel to be committed to the trust of a minister?

What can we learn from Galatians 1:10?

What do you think will happen to a spiritual leader who desires to please men?

According to John 12:42–43, what hindered some of the people and caused them *not* to confess Jesus as the Christ?

1 Thessalonians 2:5–12

> For neither at any time used we flattering words, as ye know, nor a cloke of covetousness; God is witness: nor of men sought we glory, neither of you, nor yet of others, when we might have been burdensome, as the apostles of Christ. But we were gentle among you, even as a nurse cherisheth her children: so being affectionately desirous of you, we were willing to have imparted unto you, not the gospel of God only, but also our own souls, because ye were dear unto us. For ye remember, brethren, our labour and travail: for labouring night and day, because we would not be chargeable unto any of you, we preached unto you

> the gospel of God. Ye are witnesses, and God also, how holily and justly and unblameably we behaved ourselves among you that believe: as ye know how we exhorted and comforted and charged every one of you, as a father doth his children, that ye would walk worthy of God, who hath called you unto his kingdom and glory.

In verse 5, the apostle continues to demonstrate the pureness of heart with which he ministered in Thessalonica. Paul and his companions did not aim to impress their audience with *flattering words*. Rather, they ministered with a deep heart of concern for the people of Thessalonica. Furthermore, they used no *cloak of covetousness*. This means that in no way were their true motives hidden from view! They simply did not desire money, fame, or prestige as apostles. On the contrary, instead of coming to town with a trumpet to introduce themselves as authoritative apostles to be revered, they were *gentle* among the people. They cared for the people just like a loving mother would cherish her own children. This is a picture of tenderness and real heartfelt concern for the souls of men! The apostle goes so far as to say they were willing to not only share the gospel with these dear people but to lay down their lives if necessary to reach them (v. 8).

Paul pointed out to these believers that he and his team purposely gave up the privilege of receiving any kind of compensation from the young church at Thessalonica. He determined to "not be chargeable," or to not be an expense, to any of them. Evidently the apostle saw the need at Thessalonica to avoid any appearance of wrong motives in the eyes of the people. Although he taught churches elsewhere the propriety of caring for those in the ministry, and though his motives were pure, Paul discerned the need to forego this privilege lest some falsely accuse him of wrong motives.

Paul's foremost priority was the wellbeing of these young believers, so he determined that nothing be misconstrued to hinder the work of the gospel among these people. Paul determined to maintain a testimony that was above reproach! He definitely went the second mile to ensure he lost no credibility in the eyes of the people. From Paul's perspective, his gentleness and genuine concern for the people earned him the right to be heard. He then proceeded to exhort, comfort, and direct these young believers in their walk with the Lord much like a father would his own children. He compelled them by his own example to "walk worthy of God," who called them to his kingdom and glory.

Suggested Activities

Paul did not use "flattering words" in an effort to gain an audience or to influence those who listened to him. Read 1 Corinthians 1:10–2:5. How can this passage help us as we approach a lost world with the gospel?

What lessons can pastors and laymen learn from the attitude with which Paul served the Thessalonians (vv. 5–6)?

Read Philippians 4:10–19. What did the church in Philippi do for Paul while he was in Thessalonica?

A pure motive is certainly a prerequisite if one is to be used by the Holy Spirit to touch others. Note again Paul's obvious love for these people (v. 8) and compare it to his statement in Romans 9:1–3. *What measure of concern do you have in your own heart for the lost?*

Please read Ephesians 4:1 and Colossians 1:10. These verses state the same admonition to believers as is found in verse 12 of this chapter. How do we as believers walk worthy of God?

1 Thessalonians 2:13–20

> For this cause also thank we God without ceasing, because, when ye received the word of God which ye heard of us, ye received it not as the word of men, but as it is in truth, the word of God, which effectually worketh also in you that believe. For ye, brethren,

became followers of the churches of God which in Judaea are in Christ Jesus: for ye also have suffered like things of your own countrymen, even as they have of the Jews: who both killed the Lord Jesus, and their own prophets, and have persecuted us; and they please not God, and are contrary to all men: forbidding us to speak to the Gentiles that they might be saved, to fill up their sins alway: for the wrath is come upon them to the uttermost. But we, brethren, being taken from you for a short time in presence, not in heart, endeavoured the more abundantly to see your face with great desire. Wherefore we would have come unto you, even I Paul, once and again; but Satan hindered us. For what is our hope, or joy, or crown of rejoicing? Are not even ye in the presence of our Lord Jesus Christ at his coming? For ye are our glory and joy.

You should note the attitude of the Thessalonians toward the message Paul delivered to them. They received that message not as the word of a man. Rather, they received it as it is in truth, *the Word of God!* In obedience to Christ we must carry the gospel to everyone, but the message can only effectually work in those who respect it as the Word of God. We should never attempt to win men to Christ by leaning upon human wisdom. Instead, we should share the Word of God as clearly as possible and rely solely upon the Holy Spirit to use the Word to convict those who believe.

Inasmuch as the Thessalonians received the same Word of God as the rest of the church, they were followers (or imitators) of the churches already existing in Judaea at that time. The church at Thessalonica consisted mainly of Gentile believers while the churches in Judaea consisted of mainly Jewish believers. Both groups, however, shared the same common experience of persecution at the hands of their countrymen. It is important to understand that persecution is a normal part of the Christian life. As well, while various things tend to divide the Christian community, persecution always serves to bind Christians together like nothing else can. Petty differences become insignificant in light of the suffering of those we know to be brothers in Christ.

In verse 15, the apostle Paul charged his fellow countrymen with the guilt of putting the Son of God to death! It is likely that as a young man Paul (known as Saul of Tarsus before his conversion and a former Pharisee himself) also consented to the death of Jesus. Without question, Paul understood exactly how the Jewish community largely rejected Jesus and called for his death at Pilate's hand. However, while there is a context in which the Jews rejected their Messiah and are responsible for his death, the truth is we *all* are responsible for the death of Jesus. It was for the sin of the world that he died!

In the latter part of this chapter, Paul speaks again of his love for these believers. His initial stay at Thessalonica was cut short by the opposition he received from unbelieving Jews in the city (Acts 17:1–10), so the apostle spoke of his great desire to see them again. Paul said his converts at Thessalonica were his "crown of rejoicing." What joy it is to help others come to Christ! What joy it will be in heaven to know that we had a part in helping someone to be saved. Like Paul, our own converts and those we help bring to Christ will cause great joy and rejoicing in our hearts in the presence of our Lord Jesus Christ at his coming.

Note again the apostle's declaration that Jesus is coming (v. 19). The Thessalonians turned from idols to the living God and were now waiting "for his Son from heaven" (1 Thess. 1:10). The second coming of Christ is a central part of the Christian faith. It simply is not possible to preach Christ and leave out the message of his second coming! In fact, the implication is clear that the Thessalonians turned to Christ in light of the fact that he is coming again. His coming is a great motivation to believe the gospel lest we be lost and unprepared to meet him.

Suggested Activities

Compare verse 13 of this chapter with 2 Timothy 3:16. Should Scripture be regarded as the "word of men" or as the "word of God"?

Read Matthew 21:33–46 and evaluate Paul's statement in verse 15 in light of Jesus' parable.

Compare the phrase "fill up their sins alway" in verse 16 to a similar statement found in Genesis 15:16 (Gen. 15:13–16). Although God is longsuffering, what is the lesson in these verses?

Research the destruction of the Jewish temple and the worldwide dispersion of the Jews in AD 70. Paul's statement in verse 16 that "the wrath is come upon them to the uttermost" found fulfillment just a few short years after he penned these words!

In verse 18, Paul speaks of Satan hindering him. How does Satan hinder the work of the church today?

Will you have the joy of meeting someone in heaven you led to Christ?

CHAPTER 3

1 THESSALONIANS 3

1 Thessalonians 3:1–8

> Wherefore when we could no longer forbear, we thought it good to be left at Athens alone; and sent Timotheus, our brother, and minister of God, and our fellowlabourer in the gospel of Christ, to establish you, and to comfort you concerning your faith: that no man should be moved by these afflictions: for yourselves know that we are appointed thereunto. For verily, when we were with you, we told you before that we should suffer tribulation; even as it came to pass, and ye know. For this cause, when I could no longer forbear, I sent to know your faith, lest by some means the tempter have tempted you, and our labour be in vain. But now when Timotheus came from you unto us, and brought us good tidings of your faith and charity, and that ye have good remembrance of us always, desiring greatly to see us, as we also to see you: therefore, brethren, we were comforted over you in all our affliction and distress by your faith: for now we live, if ye stand fast in the Lord.

Paul's heart for the Thessalonians is obvious in this passage. He longed to know that they were standing fast in the Lord in spite of the afflictions (pressures, tensions, difficulties) resulting from their confession of Christ. Paul had warned them while he was in Thessalonica that tribulation would come. In light of that fact, he longed to know of the sincerity of their faith, lest his labors had been in vain. Paul was greatly comforted in all of his afflictions at the word from

Timothy that the Thessalonians were not moved by the trouble they experienced at the hands of their own people (2:14). Instead they stood fast! The meaning here is that the Thessalonians "took their stand" with the Lord. How refreshing this was to the heart of the apostle Paul. He could go on with a sense of personal renewal and joy produced by the assurance that these believers were genuine.

"The tempter" Paul speaks of in verse 5 is a reference to Satan. All those who claim faith in the Lord Jesus will be tested. Satan will see to that! However, faith that is genuine will stand fast in the Lord. This is why the testing of our faith is allowed—so it "might be found unto praise and honor and glory at the appearing of Jesus Christ" (1 Peter 1:7).

Suggested Activities

Paul makes reference to the city of Athens in verse 1 of this chapter. Read Acts 17:16–34 for additional information about Paul's stay in Athens.

Read John 16:33. In this verse, what did Jesus say would happen to his disciples? (Compare this verse with Paul's teaching in verses 3 and 4 of this chapter.)

Read 2 Timothy 3:12. What did the apostle Paul insist would be normal for those who live godly in Christ Jesus? (Compare 1 Peter 4:12–19.)

Discuss this question with other Christians: How can trouble (persecution, distress, pressures, various forms of mistreatment and ridicule because of one's confession of Christ) be used of the Lord in the life of a believer?

Read the Parable of the Sower in Mark 4:1–20. Which seed pictures a professed believer who stumbles when affliction and persecution occur for the Word's sake? Which seed do you think pictures the Thessalonians?

1 Thessalonians 3:9–13

> For what thanks can we render to God again for you, for all the joy wherewith we joy for your sakes before our God; night and day praying exceedingly that we might see your face, and might perfect that which is lacking in your faith? Now God himself and our Father, and our Lord Jesus Christ, direct our way unto you. And the Lord make you to increase and abound in love one toward another, and toward all men, even as we do toward you: to the end he may stablish your hearts unblameable in holiness before God, even our Father, at the coming of our Lord Jesus Christ with all his saints.

What joy it brought to the apostle's heart to know that the Thessalonians stood fast in their faith! Paul's kinship to these believers is expressed again in his deep desire to see them and establish them further in the faith. His prayerful desire was for the Lord to make possible another visit to Thessalonica.

Please note the priorities Paul listed for their spiritual growth. First he desired that their love for one another would "increase and abound." Our love for one another as believers should result in practical actions aimed at each other's welfare. In that regard, we need to abound more and more. Next, he desired that their love for "all men" would likewise increase and abound. Those outside the church yet to come to faith in Christ need to be touched by the love of Christ *through* us. May we abound more and more!

And finally he desired that their hearts would be established unblameable in holiness before God. It is interesting to note the connection between love and holiness in this passage. Love is the real mark of maturity in the life of any believer. One cannot move on in other areas of Christian growth while lacking in love. Therefore, it is the first priority. However, abounding in love has the purpose (to the end) of helping us move on in spiritual growth in every area of our lives. That brings us to the next priority of spiritual growth: holiness.

Please note from verse 13 that holiness starts on the inside, not on the outside. It must begin in the heart. *Personal holiness develops in the walk of a believer because the heart is possessed of pure desires to please the Lord.* Godly behavior and separation from the world develop in direct proportion to a believer's personal passion to honor his or her Lord. It is possible for a believer to be "unblameable in holiness before God." The word *unblameable* carries the idea of being above reproach. We *can* serve the Lord with a heart attitude that is pure in his sight. While the outworking of personal behavior that conforms to the deep desire to please the Lord in all things will fall short of God's glory, nonetheless, as Paul states elsewhere, we can serve the law of God with our minds (Rom. 7:25). All believers should guard their hearts lest attitudes that grieve the Lord are allowed to develop and fester. God looks on the heart. Keep the condition of your heart above reproach in the sight of God. The coming of Christ and our eventual appearance with him in glory should most certainly motivate us to pure living (1 John 3:1–3).

Suggested Activities

Take a Bible concordance and look up the word *love*. Then proceed to read the passages referring to love found in the following books: Galatians, Ephesians, Philippians, Hebrews, and 1 Peter.

Read the entire book of 1 John and note the many references to love. Write down several things the Holy Spirit teaches you as you read this book.

What are some practical ways you can "abound" in love toward your brothers and sisters in Christ? Toward those who do not know the Lord?

Read 1 Peter 1:13–16. Practical holiness means that a believer is set apart to the Lord in his manner of behavior and lifestyle. Why is the attitude of heart so important to practical holiness? In what areas of your life are you struggling to conform to God's will? Do you struggle because you lack the passion to please the Lord?

Do you see from this section of 1 Thessalonians that both love and personal holiness are to be priorities in your walk with the Lord?

CHAPTER 4

1 THESSALONIANS 4

1 Thessalonians 4:1–8

> Furthermore then we beseech you, brethren, and exhort you by the Lord Jesus, that as ye have received of us how ye ought to walk and to please God, so ye would abound more and more. For ye know what commandments we gave you by the Lord Jesus. For this is the will of God, even your sanctification, that ye should abstain from fornication: that every one of you should know how to possess his vessel in sanctification and honour; not in the lust of concupiscence, even as the Gentiles which know not God: that no man go beyond and defraud his brother in any matter: because that the Lord is the avenger of all such, as we also have forewarned you and testified. For God hath not called us unto uncleanness, but unto holiness. He therefore that despiseth, despiseth not man, but God, who hath also given unto us his holy Spirit.

In this passage, the apostle Paul expounds upon the Christian ethic of sexual purity. He compels believers in every culture to conform to the moral standard of personal holiness stated in verse 3. This is the will of God, even your sanctification: that you abstain (keep yourself entirely away from) fornication. Please note that Paul exhorts us "by the Lord Jesus" to keep this command. There is no higher authority in the church than the Lord Jesus Christ. It is our Lord who calls us to this standard of personal holiness.

Therefore, we should approach the subject with the right attitude of heart. God forbid that we reject the Word of the Lord!

We should take note that the Christian ethic is in conflict with pop culture. This young church, established in one of the major cities reflecting the popular culture of that era, had to make a clear break with the accepted immorality of the day. For the most part, the gentile world did not practice the moral restraints common to Judaism and were ignorant of the Christian ethic until it was modeled by those transformed by the gospel. The walk (manner of life) of the Thessalonian believers was no longer to conform to the social norms espoused by the unbelieving world around them. Rather, God called them to holiness from uncleanness! Therefore these believers were to "abound more and more" in the personal application of these truths.

Clearly all believers must embrace the will of God taught in this chapter. We all should abstain from the practice of fornication. The Greek word *porneia* is the general word used in the New Testament for any kind of illicit sexual intercourse, prostitution, premarital sex, or adultery. Believers cannot accept these practices as social norms. Rather, we are taught to possess our vessels (bodies) in sanctification and honor. When believers save their bodies for marriage and are faithful to their husbands or wives, they "possess" their vessels (bodies) in a way that glorifies God. Christians coming out of an ungodly culture must be taught this ethic. We must be patient, but we must have the standard! In our day, we cannot accept the onslaught of immorality in any way. Marriage should be the expectation, and faithfulness in marriage should be the norm. What a testimony this is to a world that needs to know the true and living God! Such godliness stands in stark contrast to the behavior of an unbelieving world, whether in ancient Thessalonica or in our own day.

Verse 6 of this chapter must be interpreted in the context and finds immediate application to defrauding one another in the matter of unethical sexual activity. For example, believers must be content with their own spouses and should never hurt a fellow believer by violating the prohibition against adultery. This kind of behavior defrauds (robs or takes advantage of) a fellow believer. The world may routinely live with disregard for the hurt incurred by immorality, but believers are called to model a much higher standard. Failure to maintain proper respect for God's will in this matter will result in severe discipline from the Lord. Paul says that the Lord is the avenger of those in the church who defraud one another. Consider yourself forewarned, and beware of any kind of personal carelessness that might lead to this sin!

Suggested Activities

Read Acts 15:1–31. In which verses did the spiritual leadership of the early church instruct gentile believers to avoid fornication?

For discussion: How is the Christian ethic set forth in this chapter in conflict with today's popular culture? (Discuss with friends or write down your own observations.)

Use a dictionary to clarify the meaning of the word *concupiscence* found in verse 5.

In light of the teachings found in these verses, what attitude should Christians have toward pornography? Furthermore, if our society were governed by the Christian ethic found in these verses, would pornography be legal?

Read 1 Corinthians 6:15–20. What do these verses teach about the subject of fornication?

Compare 1 Corinthians 11:31–32 and Hebrews 12:5–11 with Paul's statement, "The Lord is the avenger of all such"—that is, those who indulge in fornication. Do you think it is possible for a believer to adopt the immorality of the world without consequence? Do you think a true believer will grieve over such sin? In light of God's clear indignation against this sin, shouldn't a believer be motivated to personal holiness (cf. 1 Cor. 10:6–12; Gal. 5:19–21; Rev. 9:20–21)?

Recommended resource: *Why True Love Waits* by Josh McDowell (Tyndale House Publishers). This book deals exhaustively with the problem of premarital sex and will help strengthen the resolve of all believers of all ages to maintain sexual purity.

1 Thessalonians 4:9–12

> But as touching brotherly love ye need not that I write unto you: for ye yourselves are taught of God to love one another. And indeed ye do it toward all the brethren which are in all Macedonia: but we beseech you, brethren, that ye increase more and more; and that ye study to be quiet, and to do your own business, and to work with your own hands, as we commanded you; that ye may walk honestly toward them that are without, and that ye may have lack of nothing.

In these verses, the apostle gives the church several practical principles to guide everyday life. These principles will increase to more godliness and should be followed carefully. While the church already understood the need to love one another, the apostle pleaded with them to "increase more and more!" As the apostle Peter states elsewhere, believers are to maintain a "fervent charity" amongst themselves (1 Peter 4:8). Brotherly love should be the trademark of all believers and is the indication of real maturity in a believer (Col. 3:14).

The next principle stated in verse 11 compels us to live quietly (study or *desire* to live peaceably; cf. Rom.12:18). All believers must guard against the temptation to meddle in strife (Prov. 26:17). Wise believers will "mind their own business" and offer advice only when called upon to do so. Furthermore, making oneself available to help with a legitimate need should be coupled with the discernment to respect an individual's private business.

There is another important thought connected to the statement, "Do your own business." It is the idea of personal responsibility. Believers are to work with their own hands and take care of their personal affairs in a responsible way. The irresponsible handling of personal business affairs will inevitably be a poor testimony to those outside the church. We must deal honestly with all men. Furthermore, failure to maintain a strong work ethic will lead to dependency on others for basic needs. Instead, believers are challenged to maintain self-sufficiency under normal circumstances. Obviously there are instances when an individual or family may deal with situations that present needs beyond their immediate ability to satisfy. While self-sufficiency is in view here as compared to irresponsible living, we must maintain honest professions in the interest of meeting our own personal needs and caring for those who face legitimate needs beyond their means (Eph. 4:28, Acts 20:35).

Suggested Activities

List several ways in which you can "increase more and more" in love toward fellow believers.

How do we reconcile the instruction to live quiet, peaceable lives with involvement in public affairs? Is it ever appropriate for Christians to participate in a riot?

Based upon the instruction in 1 Thessalonians 4:11–12, how would you define the Christian work ethic?

Should the promise of Christ's return ever be used to neglect good work habits?

In what ways do believers act irresponsibly today that could result in personal needs going unmet?

Is there anyone with whom you need to make restitution because of failure to follow through in personal business matters (unpaid debt, etc.)? What kind of testimony could this be to someone who is lost?

1 Thessalonians 4:13–18

> But I would not have you to be ignorant, brethren, concerning them which are asleep, that ye sorrow not, even as others which have no hope. For if we believe that Jesus died and rose again, even so them also which sleep in Jesus will God bring with him. For this we say unto you by the word of the Lord, that we which

> are alive and remain unto the coming of the Lord shall not prevent them which are asleep. For the Lord himself shall descend from heaven with a shout, with the voice of the archangel, and with the trump of God: and the dead in Christ shall rise first: then we which are alive and remain shall be caught up together with them in the clouds, to meet the Lord in the air: and so shall we ever be with the Lord. Wherefore comfort one another with these words.

There are two things about this passage that immediately stand out. First, the apostle intended to help believers understand what happens to loved ones who pass away before the Lord's return. Second, the event prophesied in these verses is monumental in its scope! What is taught in these verses amounts to one of the most significant events yet to unfold in human history. These verses declare in unmistakable language that Jesus Christ is returning for the purpose of resurrecting the bodies of departed believers and to translate living believers at that moment directly into his presence. Believers are assured by these words that departed loved ones who knew Christ are now in the presence of the Lord, that the Lord will bring them *with him* at the moment of his return, that they will receive resurrected bodies, that living believers will be *caught up* together with them in a happy reunion, and that the church will ever be with the Lord! Indeed, what comfort and hope the promise of this event has provided for each generation of believers awaiting the imminent return of the Lord Jesus.

Let's consider carefully the first point made in the paragraph above. The young believers in Thessalonica turned from their idols to "serve the living and true God, and to wait for his Son from heaven" (1:10). The promise of the return of Jesus Christ for his people filled the Thessalonians with expectation and anticipation. However, in short order, some of these believers died, and the young church needed additional instruction to answer the question as to what happened to these loved ones. The loss of a loved one is always difficult, but the apostle Paul said that they need not sorrow without hope. In fact, the believer who is absent from the body is immediately present with the Lord (2 Cor. 5:8). While the body is said to "sleep," departed loved ones are in the presence of the Lord, where they await the resurrection at Christ's coming. Furthermore, at this great event living believers have the assurance they will be reunited with those who died in Jesus. This great promise comforted the Thessalonians and answered their question. Likewise, every living generation of believers to this present time finds the same comfort and hope in these powerful words.

It is interesting to note that this passage not only answers a very important question about departed loved ones, but it is also striking in its implications. This passage describes a global event that will most certainly shake the world emotionally, physically, and financially. The world lies in spiritual darkness and will be overtaken by this event like a thief in the night. They will have no explanation for the obvious disappearance of multitudes of people who simply vanish all over the earth. Perhaps for some this event will be a wakeup call to trust Christ as Savior during the succeeding days of turmoil and upheaval predicted by many Scriptures. One thing is sure: this "catching away" or "rapture" of living believers will be yet another witness to the world of the authenticity of God's written Word. When viewed from this perspective, the rapture is not only the realization of our blessed hope (Titus 2:13), but it serves also as another demonstration of God's grace toward a world that desperately needs to believe the gospel.

The Rapture Compared to Other Major World Events

The original creation (one man from the dust)	The rapture (many from the dust!)
The translation of one man, Enoch	The translation of all living believers
The global impact of Noah's flood	The worldwide impact of millions missing
The dispersion of Babel in confusion	Our gathering together unto him in his Father's house
The resurrection of Christ (first fruits)	The resurrection of the church (those who are Christ's at his coming)

Suggested Activities

Read 1 Corinthians 15 and note verses 51 through 54 for comparison to 1 Thessalonians 4:13–18. What should we learn from verse 51? Compare verse 51 with 1 Thessalonians 4:17.

Note: The rapture should not be confused with the glorious appearing of our Lord Jesus Christ described in Revelation 19 and in other passages of Scripture. The rapture is the *first phase* of the second coming of Christ and concerns the church, the bride of Christ. A very helpful resource to use in your personal studies is the book *Charting the End Times* by Tim Lahaye and Thomas Ice. It is available from Harvest House Publishers.

Note: On page 44 is a quote from *Charting the End Times.* This information will help you see the contrast between the rapture and the glorious appearing.

Read 2 Corinthians 4:16–5:8 for more insight into the death of believers.

Have you ever heard someone set a date for the rapture of the church? Please read the words of Christ in Matthew 24:36–44. What conclusion should we draw about setting dates for the rapture?

How should the promise of Christ's return affect your life?

The apostle Paul concluded this prophetic portion of his letter to the Thessalonians with instruction to allow the truth of Christ's return for the church to comfort their hearts. Indeed, we are to *comfort one another* with these words!

The Fifteen Differences between the Rapture and the Glorious Appearing[1]

Rapture/ Blessed Hope	*Glorious Appearing*
1. Christ comes in the air for his own	1. Christ comes with his own to earth
2. Rapture of all Christians	2. No one raptured
3. Christians taken to the Father's house	3. Resurrected saints do not see the Father's house
4. No judgment on earth	4. Christ judges inhabitants of earth
5. Church taken to heaven	5. Christ sets up his kingdom on earth
6. Imminent—could happen any moment	6. Cannot occur for at least seven years
7. No signs	7. Many signs for Christ's physical coming
8. For believers only	8. Affects all humanity
9. Time of joy	9. Time of mourning
10. Before the "day of wrath" (tribulation)	10. Immediately after tribulation (Matthew 24)
11. No mention of Satan	11. Satan bound in abyss for one thousand years
12. The judgment seat of Christ	12. No time or place for judgment seat
13. Marriage of the Lamb	13. His bride descends with Him
14. Only his own see him	14. Every eye will see Him
15. Tribulation begins	15. Thousand-year kingdom of Christ begins

1 *Charting the End Times* by Tim Lahaye and Thomas Ice

The Day of the Lord

The rapture is the event that begins the day of the Lord.

It includes the tribulation (the seventieth week of Daniel's prophecy).

It includes the judgment of Christ upon the nations at his glorious appearing.

It includes the millennial kingdom (the day of Christ)

The day of the Lord concludes with the catastrophic end of this present order and the introduction of a new heaven and a new earth.

Suggested Activity

The expression "that day" or "the day" or "the great day" occurs more than seventy-five times in the Old Testament. Read these related Scriptures for more study: Daniel 9:16–27; Matthew 25:31–46; 2 Thessalonians 2:2; Isaiah 2:12, 13:6, 9; Ezekiel 30:1–3; Joel 1:15, 2:1, 11, 31, 3:12–17; Amos 5:18–20; Obadiah 15; Zephaniah 1:7, 14–18; Zechariah 14:1–9; Malachi 4:5; Acts 2:14–21; 2 Peter 3:9–13.

CHAPTER 5

1 THESSALONIANS 5

1 Thessalonians 5:1–11

> But of the times and the seasons, brethren, ye have no need that I write unto you. For yourselves know perfectly that the day of the Lord so cometh as a thief in the night. For when they shall say, Peace and safety; then sudden destruction cometh upon them, as travail upon a woman with child; and they shall not escape. But ye, brethren, are not in darkness, that that day should overtake you as a thief. Ye are all the children of light, and the children of the day: we are not of the night, nor of darkness. Therefore let us not sleep, as do others; but let us watch and be sober. For they that sleep sleep in the night; and they that be drunken are drunken in the night. But let us, who are of the day, be sober, putting on the breastplate of faith and love; and for an helmet, the hope of salvation. For God hath not appointed us to wrath, but to obtain salvation by our Lord Jesus Christ, who died for us, that, whether we wake or sleep, we should live together with him. Wherefore comfort yourselves together, and edify one another, even as also ye do.

The beginning of chapter 5 is connected to the apostle's discussion of the rapture in the previous chapter. In fact, it was necessary for Paul to write to the Thessalonians and clarify the details of the rapture since that event is not discussed in the Old Testament. The rapture is said to be a "mystery" (1 Cor. 15:51), which is to say it was a truth hidden from the view of the Old Testament prophets. Thus, it was necessary to write to the church and reveal the great truth of the rapture for those generations connected to the approach of the Lord's return for his bride, the church. However, with regard to the times and seasons connected to the coming "day of the Lord," there was no need to provide new revelation since this great day is the central theme of the Old Testament prophets. Even an elementary understanding of the Old Testament Scripture would have provided the Thessalonians with an understanding that the day of the Lord was coming! Thus, Paul had no specific need to write to them about that part of God's prophetic program.

Verse 2 reveals that the coming events constituting the day of the Lord will catch the world by surprise like a thief in the night. A comparable season of world history occurred during the days of Noah. Although Noah's life and message cried out to his generation that the flood was coming, the people of his day went about business as usual until the flood came and took them all away (Matt. 24:37–39). Likewise the coming day of the Lord will be a period of world history not anticipated by those in unbelief. Blinded by unbelief, even following the rapture of the church the world will embrace a false spirituality, which will include a supposed program of peace. However, the dreams of world peace will end in sudden destruction!

Verse 3 alludes to the great theme of peace and safety

that will be touted by the coming man of sin, the antichrist. This last world ruler, who will be the head of the coming new world order, will make a peace treaty that will seemingly resolve the crisis between Israel and the nations of the world. He will secure Israel for a short time and avoid an all-out world war for a brief season. Then, just as travail overtakes a woman with child, the world will be plunged into utter chaos and destruction. It should be pointed out that this destruction will not simply be the natural result of war between the nations. Rather, it will include the specific judgments of the Lord that characterize the coming day of the Lord. The world will not escape this coming judgment!

Paul hastens to point out that we are not in darkness, that that day should overtake us as a thief. We are children of the light. This means we understand exactly what is coming. Those born of God's Spirit generally see the prophetic future clearly. Consequently, the rapture and the succeeding day of the Lord will come as no surprise to us at all. On the contrary, the promise of the Lord's return is our blessed hope and a source of great joy in our hearts.

With that said, we should take careful note of the exhortation the Holy Spirit gives in verses 5 through 8. In light of our Lord's return, we are to maintain a spiritual state of alertness. We are not to sleep but to watch and be of serious mind. If we honestly believe the rapture and the succeeding day of the Lord are coming, then we should serve the Lord with fervent hearts. Let us who are of the day put on the breastplate of faith and love and the helmet of salvation (cf. Eph. 6:14–17). The point is, those who are of the day should be engaged in spiritual warfare until the Lord comes. In no way should we succumb to the spirit of this world by compromising the truth of God's Word. Rather, we are to remain faithful witnesses of the truth until the day of our catching away to be with the Lord! Regardless of the indifference of many and perhaps the mocking of many others, let us remain true and faithful to our Lord Jesus Christ until he comes.

Verse 9 contains an important truth that bears careful consideration. God has not appointed his church to wrath but to obtain salvation through our Lord Jesus Christ. In light of the fact that the coming day of the Lord (also known as the tribulation period, the seventieth week of Daniel's prophecy) is a time of the Lord's wrath and indignation, this verse indicates that the church will not be present as this period of world history unfolds. Study this statement carefully in the greater context of Bible prophecy. It is evident that all the saved will escape the eternal wrath of God expressed in *gehenna* (the lake of fire, Rev. 20:14–15), but this verse is not speaking of that wrath. Rather, it speaks of escaping the wrath of God that is a part of the coming day of the Lord. This statement lends support for a *pretribulation* rapture of the church.

Again, the teaching of Christ's second coming should be a source of comfort and edification for all believers during the entire church age (vv. 10–11).

1 Thessalonians 5:12-15

> And we beseech you, brethren, to know them which labour among you, and are over you in the Lord, and admonish you; and to esteem them very highly in love for their work's sake. And be at peace among yourselves. Now we exhort you, brethren, warn them that are unruly, comfort the feebleminded, support the weak, be patient toward all men. See that none render evil for evil unto any man; but ever follow that which is good, both among yourselves, and to all men.

The last section of chapter 5 is filled with practical commands for the church. We can profit greatly when we apply this instruction to our lives. In verses 12 and 13, the apostle encourages believers to recognize those who are over them in the Lord. This speaks of pastors and elders in the church who are known for their labor, especially the work of ministering the Word of God to the people. They are to be treated very well in love for their work's sake.

Next the apostle teaches us to be at peace with one another in the church. This certainly applies to individual congregations, but we must also apply this command to the greater body of Christ. It is not becoming for professed Christians to be at strife with one another. Disagreements should be handled graciously and in the Spirit of Christ. Patient love toward those who are not a part of our immediate congregation will maintain an appropriate testimony before a watching world!

Verse 14 provides more guidance for the life of a congregation. First it says we are to warn the unruly. Insubordination is in view here. Every believer needs to maintain a simple respect for order in the church. Generally believers should maintain a respect for spiritual leadership. Of course, spiritual leaders are most certainly accountable to the church. However, if such leaders maintain their testimony, provide a mature example for other believers, and are doctrinally sound, then it is not in order for a believer to be disgruntled. Unruly behavior inevitably stirs up unnecessary strife. Another point to be made here concerns unruly behavior that is not consistent with one's profession of faith. We are to walk in the Spirit! Unwillingness to submit to the clear will of God is unruly behavior. Those in the Christian community who openly rebel against the clear teaching of Scripture are to be warned!

We are also taught in verse 14 to comfort the feebleminded (the fainthearted) and support the weak. The fainthearted speaks of those who are "low in spirit." Another word for this condition is depressed. Obviously there are different reasons why a believer may be discouraged, low in spirit, or depressed. Sometimes a believer passes through a season of life or a certain spiritual battle that causes depression. Sometimes an individual struggles regularly with faintheartedness. In either case, we are to comfort fellow believers who are dealing with this condition.

Along this line, we are also called to support the weak. It seems most likely that this statement refers to the *spiritually* weak. We are to come alongside such believers and offer support in the form of brotherly friendship. It is not possible to support the weak without personal contact with the individual in need. We need to take a personal interest in those who need to grow spiritually. It follows that creating appropriate settings for interaction is necessary if we are to support the weak. This may take the form of personal friendship, or the church as a whole could implement group opportunities for teaching and fellowship.

Verse 14 concludes with the instruction to be patient with all men! This includes those in the church *and* those outside the fellowship of the church. It is interesting to note that we only need to exercise patience with others when their behavior disappoints us in some way. This command is a challenge! Quite frankly, it is doubtful we will ever *feel* like extending patience toward anyone. It is at the very moment of disappointment that the Spirit calls us to "put up with" the person who is at fault! The demonstration of patience toward those around us is certainly a mark of spiritual maturity. It is undoubtedly the love of Christ at work in us that produces patience.

Verse 15 follows with the instruction *not* to render evil for evil. This verse reflects the similar teaching of the apostle in Romans 12:17–21. Christians must never adopt the spirit of this world! We are not to seek revenge. Rather, we are to overcome evil with good. Let the Spirit of Christ shape your attitude. Do good even to your enemy! Adhering to this high standard of behavior is a powerful witness for Christ, but such behavior is not natural to us. However, the indwelling Holy Spirit will enable us to overcome evil with good as He leads us to embrace the Spirit of Christ.

Suggested Activities

How should believers treat spiritual leaders (1 Thess. 5:12–13)? Read these passages for further study: 1 Timothy 4:11–16; Hebrews 13:7, 17; 1 Peter 5:1–3.

In what ways can we practice being at peace with one another?

Cite an example of unruly behavior.

How do we comfort the feeble hearted?

In what practical ways can we support the spiritually weak?

1 Thessalonians 5:16–28

> Rejoice evermore. Pray without ceasing. In everything give thanks: for this is the will of God in Christ Jesus concerning you. Quench not the Spirit. Despise not prophesyings. Prove all things; hold fast that which is good. Abstain from all appearance of evil. And the very God of peace sanctify you wholly; and I pray God your whole spirit and soul and body be preserved blameless unto the coming of our Lord Jesus Christ. Faithful is he that calleth you, who also will do it. Brethren, pray for us. Greet all the brethren with an holy kiss. I charge you by the Lord that this epistle be read unto all the holy brethren. The grace of our Lord Jesus Christ be with you. Amen.

This section of chapter 5 is filled with more-practical commands. Each command contributes to the believer's spiritual life. Consequently, we need to take them to heart and profit as a result. The first command is to "rejoice evermore." The wellspring of joy for the believer is the possession of eternal life! Isaiah 61:10 states it this way: "I will greatly rejoice in the Lord, my soul shall be joyful in my God; for he hath clothed me with the garments of salvation, he hath covered me with the robe of righteousness, as a bridegroom decketh himself with ornaments, and as a bride adorneth herself with her jewels." Praise the Lord! The free gift of eternal life by faith in Jesus Christ our Lord is to be the source of daily rejoicing in the Lord (cf. Phil. 4:4).

Next we are taught to pray without ceasing. Don't cease from the habit of praying. Prayer is the privilege of every believer. We are invited to come boldly to the throne of grace in prayer! Furthermore, we must pray without ceasing in the sense that we keep on asking until we receive (cf. Matt. 7:7).

The next command is also related to our prayer life. Scripture teaches us to give thanks in everything. Notice this verse does not say we are to be thankful *for* everything but *in* everything. Here the Holy Spirit is teaching us to maintain a thankful heart through all the experiences we encounter in life. Life has it trials, but the Lord assures us that he is working all things together for our good (Rom. 8:28). While all things are not good, what a wonderful consolation it is to know that the Lord is *working* all things together *for* our good! Consequently, a thankful heart can be maintained through every situation. As well, a thankful heart learns to count its blessings even while dealing with trials so as not to forget all the Lord's benefits.

Notice the next command, which says, "Quench not the Spirit." The Holy Spirit is at work in the life of every believer. He produces godly conviction in the heart. As well, he *calls* the believer to serve with passion. Such fire in a believer's heart is not to be extinguished. In most instances, it is quite normal to quench or put out a fire by any means possible.

However, in the case of the Spirit's work in our heart, we are *not* to put that fire out! Quench not the Spirit! Let him have his way with you. Follow the Lord's lead in your life with passion.

In verse 20 we read, "Despise not prophesyings." The general meaning of prophesying is to speak God's Word in the power of the Holy Spirit. Sometimes there is a predictive element involved, but the usage here is more inclusive. Anytime the Word of God is preached, the minister is prophesying. Since the preached Word generally involves correction of some sort, we must guard against "despising" (holding in contempt or showing disrespect for) the preached Word. Rather, we are to prepare ourselves for change.

The next command in verse 21 is of great importance. We are to prove or test all things. After proper examination, we are to hold fast that which is good. The text assumes that we understand an objective standard exists by which we can measure all things. That standard is the written Word of God! We are to test all things against Scripture. It follows that we must reject all teaching unsupported by the Word of God! The most important application of this admonition is to test the spirits. Any spirit that refuses to confess the unique nature of Jesus the Christ as revealed in Scripture must be firmly rejected (cf. 1 John 4:1–6). This instruction in verse 21 is a call to spiritual discernment. We are not to be spiritually gullible. Too much is at stake simply to accept all things of a spiritual nature. Therefore, we are compelled to prove all things for the purpose of identifying that which is good. We should cleave to that which is good and soundly reject that which is evil.

The next command found in this passage says, "Abstain from all appearance of evil." This verse compels us to go the second mile in maintaining our testimony for Christ. Our behavior needs to be above reproach. Careless behavior can give the impression of wrongdoing even though no misconduct has occurred. Remember this: we are to function as the light of the world. We do so by sharing the truth verbally, but a sound testimony necessarily adds integrity to our efforts. Sloppy habits will be a hindrance to our witness for Christ so avoid even the appearance of wrongdoing. A second thought from this verse applies to avoiding temptation. The wise believer learns to avoid social settings that can quickly evolve into personal failure.

Please notice the reference to the nature of man in verse 23. Clearly man consists of a material body and an immaterial soul/spirit. Our Lord will preserve our complete being unto his heavenly kingdom. Our salvation includes deliverance from our lost condition in hell and the redemption of our bodies at his coming, thus the prayer for our whole spirits, souls, and bodies to be preserved until he comes. The Lord is faithful and will perform all the promises connected to our salvation (v. 24).

The epistle closes with the instruction to pray for the apostle. In fact, all spiritual leaders need the fervent prayers of the church. Practice prayer on behalf of your pastor (s) and other spiritual leaders in your life. This is much needed, and the Lord will use it to prosper his work.

Verse 27 still applies to us today. This epistle (along with the rest of Holy Scripture) is to be read to all the holy brethren. How we need to go carefully through books of the Bible verse by verse! This is a necessary practice in the life of any congregation.

Suggested Activities

How do you think the practice of verse 18 will affect your life?

If the Holy Spirit is building a fire in another believer, do you think we could be guilty of dumping a bucket of water on his or her fire? How?

Is it easier for believers to engage in other areas of their walk than to allow the preached Word to change them?

Can you cite an example of something spiritual you tested against Scripture and found it untrue or otherwise not good for you?

Why should Christians go the second mile to maintain their testimony?

CHAPTER 6

2 THESSALONIANS 1

2 Thessalonians 1:1–3

> Paul, and Silvanus, and Timotheus, unto the church of the Thessalonians in God our Father and the Lord Jesus Christ: grace unto you, and peace, from God our Father and the Lord Jesus Christ. We are bound to thank God always for you, brethren, as it is meet, because that your faith groweth exceedingly, and the charity of every one of you all toward each other aboundeth;

The second epistle to the Thessalonians followed not long after Paul's first letter to the church. It appears that the main reason for the letter was to correct spurious teachings about the return of Christ that began circulating among the Thessalonians in Paul's name (cf. 2 Thess. 2:1). The church at Thessalonica was enduring persecution. Evidently under the influence of misguided instruction, the church thought the rapture had occurred and they were now in the tribulation period. However, Paul corrected this misguided thinking in chapter 2 of this letter.

As was the case in his first letter, Paul opened this epistle with an acknowledgment of his coworkers Silas and Timothy. He proceeded to write unto the church of the Thessalonians, which was "in God our Father and the Lord Jesus Christ." All believers now abide in a personal relationship to the Father (cf. 1 John 3:1). This relationship as adopted children is predicated upon personal faith in the Lord Jesus Christ. Those reconciled to God by faith in Christ are indeed *in* God our Father and the Lord Jesus Christ! This speaks of the wonderful security that is the birthright of every child of God.

Paul went on to speak of grace and peace in his introduction to the church. We should note that after conversion, the Father continues to lavish grace upon his redeemed. In fact, he will show us the riches of his grace throughout the eternal ages to come (cf. Eph. 2:7). How appropriate it is to declare "grace and peace" unto believers from God the Father and the Lord Jesus Christ! Note also that personal peace comes to the heart *after* one is saved by grace. Peace follows grace. It is quite evident to me from personal experience that this is the order of things in one's spiritual life. A greater understanding of grace by a believer always results in a greater measure of personal peace in the heart of that believer. I pray also that grace and peace be multiplied to you from your heavenly Father and his Son, the Lord Jesus Christ!

You will recall that the Thessalonians turned from idols to serve the Lord Jesus Christ upon hearing the gospel preached by Paul. The strong testimony of this church was widespread at that time. As Paul wrote this second letter, he was pleased to note how their faith continued to grow exceedingly, and as a result, their love toward one another continued to abound. Although this church needed additional instruction concerning the details of the return of Christ, their testimony for the Lord was not lacking. In fact, their example is a model for churches today. Like the Thessalonians, let us pursue a growing faith and a love that abounds more and more. Such churches are a powerful testimony to the world around them.

Suggested Activities

Read John 10:25–30. How does this passage relate to the teaching found in verse 1 that states we are "in God our Father and the Lord Jesus Christ"?

How would you define a faith that is growing exceedingly?

In what practical ways can our love toward one another abound?

2 Thessalonians 1:4–6

> So that we ourselves glory in you in the churches of God for your patience and faith in all your persecutions and tribulations that ye endure: which is a manifest token of the righteous judgment of God, that ye may be counted worthy of the kingdom of God, for which ye also suffer: seeing it is a righteous thing with God to recompense tribulation to them that trouble you;

It is obvious that the apostle Paul found great joy in the mighty work of the Spirit among the Thessalonian people. Paul often spoke of this mighty work as he moved among the other churches of God. He gloried in them, or said another way, he boasted about their example to the other churches. Not only did they turn from idols to serve the living God and his Son, the Lord Jesus Christ, but they also continued faithfully in spite of persecutions and tribulations. It was appropriate for the apostle to call attention to such a strong example of Christian faith.

As we noted earlier, the Thessalonians endured persecution and tribulation at the hands of their own countrymen. This is a graphic reminder of exactly what the Lord Jesus taught us to expect from the world. In the gospel of St. John, the Lord Jesus said:

> If the world hate you, ye know that it hated me before it hated you. If ye were of the world, the world would love his own: but because ye are not of the world, but I have chosen you out of the world, therefore the world hateth you. Remember the word that I said unto you, The servant is not greater than his lord. If they have persecuted me, they will also persecute you; if they have kept my saying, they will keep yours also. But all these things will they do unto you for my name's sake, because they know not him that sent me … These things have I spoken unto you, that ye should not be

> offended. They shall put you out of the synagogues: yea, the time cometh, that whosoever killeth you will think that he doeth God service. And these things will they do unto you, because they have not known the Father, nor me. But these things have I told you, that when the time shall come, ye may remember that I told you of them. And these things I said not unto you at the beginning, because I was with you ... These things I have spoken unto you, that in me ye might have peace. In the world ye shall have tribulation: but be of good cheer; I have overcome the world. (John 15:18–21; 16:1–4, 33)

Jesus clearly taught that his disciples would experience tribulation or trouble in this world. This means it is common for believers to experience opposition to their faith. The opposition experienced is for *his name's sake* and comes from those who do not know him or his Father. It is important for every disciple of the Lord Jesus to understand that persecution and tribulation is a *normal* part of our experience as we confess Christ and seek to win others to him (cf. 1 Peter 4:12–14).

Please note the perspective found on suffering in verse 5 of this chapter. God does allow his people to suffer for his name's sake, and this is a manifestation of "the righteous judgment of God." Indeed, we are not above our Master! From God's perspective, faithfulness on the part of those who endure suffering for the name of Jesus counts them as worthy of the kingdom of God. While suffering does not *make* us worthy of entrance into the kingdom (only the blood of Christ has the power to do that), nonetheless suffering saints are counted worthy of all the future glory to be revealed in them. In Romans 8:18 we read, "For I reckon that the sufferings of this present time are not worthy to be compared with the glory which shall be revealed in us." Praise the Lord! Those who suffer with Christ are worthy to reign with him (cf. 2 Tim. 2:12). In light of this truth, it is the greatest of all privileges to suffer for the name of Jesus.

In this present hour, the righteous are often persecuted and mistreated, sometimes even unto death. But the current scenario is not the end of the story! In fact, the day will come when the Lord will recompense tribulation to those who trouble the saints (v. 6). In other words, the Lord is going to give those who trouble the saints (persecute and oppose them) some of their own medicine. In Revelation 16:4–7, we see this principle graphically illustrated during the coming great tribulation. Those who shed the blood of the saints will be recompensed with blood to drink!

2 Thessalonians 1:7–12

> And to you who are troubled rest with us, when the Lord Jesus shall be revealed from heaven with his mighty angels, in flaming fire taking vengeance on them that know not God, and that obey not the gospel of our Lord Jesus Christ: who shall be punished with everlasting destruction from the presence of the Lord, and from the glory of his power; when he shall come to be glorified in his saints, and to be admired in all them that believe (because our testimony among you was believed) in that day. Wherefore also we pray always for you, that our God would count you worthy of this calling, and fulfill all the good pleasure of his goodness, and the work of faith with power: that the name of our Lord Jesus Christ may be glorified in you, and ye in him, according to the grace of our God and the Lord Jesus Christ.

In verse 7, Paul continues the thought of verse 6. Believers who experience tribulation and persecution are to find their comfort in the fact that the Lord Jesus will one day balance the scales of justice. The day will come when the Lord Jesus will return in great power and glory to take vengeance on those who know not God and who refuse to obey the gospel. The word *vengeance* as used here speaks of satisfying justice in righteousness. The world will discover that the Lord gives justice to the unrepentant. Woe to the man who must face the righteous Judge and receive recompense for the wrongs committed! Persecution may be a reality for most believers, but it is an injustice committed by those who know not God. The perpetrators will one day face the Lord Jesus and give account of the wrongs committed against his people. The Thessalonians were to understand that their rest would come and trouble would cease (cf. Rev. 6:9–11, 14:12–13).

Verse 7 speaks clearly about the revelation of the Lord Jesus Christ (cf. Matt. 24:29–31, 25:31–32; Rev. 19:11–16). The visible return of Jesus Christ to literally rule and reign on earth is a cardinal truth of Scripture. While his return is characterized in verse 8 as a day of "flaming fire" in which he judges unbelief, it will also mean the establishment of his glorious kingdom (cf. Isa. 9:6–7; 11:9–10; Zech. 14:9).

Verse 8 is a powerful statement about the severity of God's judgment upon those who reject the knowledge of God and who refuse to obey the gospel of our Lord Jesus Christ. Those who "know not God" are not ignorant of his existence or his will. Rather, they are not reconciled to God by faith in his Son. They rejected the love and mercy available to all who choose to repent. Consequently, they lack a personal relationship to God and must face his indignation. As the Scripture says, "And he that believeth not the Son shall not see life; but the wrath of God abideth on him" (John 3:36b).

Again in verse 8, take careful note of the failure of the

lost to "obey the gospel of our Lord Jesus Christ." Obedience to the gospel entails turning away from all false spirituality. Repentance is inherent in the gospel. Upon hearing the gospel, one is compelled by the truth to forsake one's false gods and every false way. Thus the gospel calls us to repentance! Furthermore, the gospel seeks to conquer the heart by the power of Christ's love demonstrated at the cross. Obedience to the gospel means that one responds to the manifest love of Christ with a yielded heart. Once the heart is yielded in repentance, the believer is willing to trust Christ as Savior and confess that Jesus is the Lord! It is in this sense the gospel must be obeyed. I repeat: *God's command to believe upon his Son must be obeyed*! Failure to honor the Lord with obedience to the gospel is exactly why the wrath of God is coming on the world (cf. Heb. 10:26–31).

Verse 9 describes the divine retribution as "everlasting destruction" from the presence of the Lord. Those who refuse to repent and turn to Christ will suffer eternal, conscious separation from the presence of the Lord. The lake of fire is the final place of eternal separation from the Lord. It is a place of wailing, weeping, and gnashing of teeth. There is no rest in this place of darkness. The soul will forever experience the express wrath of God that burns eternally. My friend, as long as God remains on the throne with the song of redemption filling heaven with glory and praise to his great name, that's how long the groans and sorrows of the darkened regions of the damned will grind on! Knowing the terror of the Lord, we persuade men! It is always of the greatest importance that immediately upon hearing the gospel one responds with obedience to the call of Christ. In so doing one escapes the second death and will not perish everlastingly.

Paul concluded this section of his letter with a word of encouragement to the Thessalonians. He assured them that he was praying for them. Specifically he prayed that they would be counted "worthy of this calling." Said another way, the Thessalonians were to bear the name of Jesus well. And so is every believer. We are to glorify the name of the Lord Jesus Christ! Failure to do so falls short of our calling. Believers who practice a separated life from the world and who pursue personal holiness in their behavior are walking worthy of God (cf. Eph. 4:1, 5:1–17; 1 Peter 1:14–16).

If you are a Christian, then bear the family name well. Don't be an embarrassment to your heavenly Father or the rest of the family! Be concerned about the Father's evaluation of your behavior as a believer. God's approval is all that matters. It should be your desire to have God's smile of approval. If you have his smile of approval, then he counts you worthy of this calling! You are glorifying his name.

Suggested Activities

Consider acquiring the following two books for your personal library: *The Coming Kingdom of Christ* by the late evangelist John Rice and *The Late Great Planet Earth* by Hal Lindsey. Direct any questions you have about these two resources to: askPastorRusty@cbmtoday.org.

Using a *Strong's Bible Concordance,* look up the word *hell*, and read each passage in the gospels of Matthew, Mark, Luke, and John that contain the word. As you read, note what Jesus taught about hell.

CHAPTER 7
2 THESSALONIANS 2

2 Thessalonians 2:1–5

> Now we beseech you, brethren, by the coming of our Lord Jesus Christ, and by our gathering together unto him, that ye be not soon shaken in mind, or be troubled, neither by spirit, nor by word, nor by letter as from us, as that the day of Christ is at hand. Let no man deceive you by any means: for that day shall not come, except there come a falling away first, and that man of sin be revealed, the son of perdition; who opposeth and exalteth himself above all that is called God, or that is worshipped; so that he as God sitteth in the temple of God, shewing himself that he is God. Remember ye not, that, when I was yet with you, I told you these things?

This chapter delves into the main reason Paul wrote a second letter to the Thessalonians. He intended to clarify a very important detail concerning the second coming of the Lord Jesus Christ. Paul began this chapter with a reference to the event detailed in 1 Thessalonians 4:13–18 when he spoke of "our gathering together unto him" in verse 1. This *gathering together unto him* is what we commonly refer to as *the rapture*. At that momentous event, living believers will be reunited with their departed loved ones as the church experiences the redemption of the body.

The focus of the rapture is the *resurrection* of the church, which includes two supernatural aspects. First, the creative power of God will clothe the departed church with glorified bodies called forth from the dust of the earth. Next, the part of the church that is alive and remaining at the coming of the Lord will be changed in a moment's time! The mortal, corruptible bodies of believers alive at Christ's coming must be transformed by the resurrection power of the living God. This "gathering together unto him" with our departed loved ones is the *blessed hope* intended to comfort all believers since the day of our Lord's ascension into heaven (cf. Titus 2:11–14).

However, the Thessalonians evidently were shaken and troubled in mind that they were entering that period of time known as "the day of Christ" or the day of the Lord. As the apostle Paul indicates in verse 2, someone (another teacher or perhaps a group of fellow believers) came behind him and suggested that the notable day of the Lord was unfolding. Of course, this would either mean that the rapture already occurred (leaving the Thessalonians and others behind) or that there is no such thing as the rapture after all. No wonder the Thessalonians lost the comfort Paul speaks of in 1 Thessalonians 4:18! They were now "shaken in mind" and "troubled" (v. 2). At this point, the apostle very clearly outlined the order of events associated with the second coming of the Lord with the aim of calming the minds of the Thessalonian believers.

In verse 3, Paul clearly teaches that the day of Christ *will not* occur until two things happen. First, there must be a *falling away.* And second, the *man of sin* must be revealed. As the Thessalonians studied this corrective word from the apostle Paul, they immediately recognized that the day of Christ was *not* upon them! This was the logical conclusion because the "falling away" and the appearance of the "man of sin" had not yet occurred. Thus their fears were unfounded. In effect, Paul restored to the heart of the Thessalonians the "blessed hope" that the doctrinal truth of the rapture provides for those believers who understand it.

This restoration of comfort to the hearts of the Thessalonians was immediate and lasting as they embraced Paul's message contained in the phrase "falling away first." There are only two suggested meanings of this phrase as translators work with the Greek language. First, in the early English translations of the New Testament (from the 1384 Wycliffe Bible until the Geneva Bible of 1608) the text read "except there come a *departing first.*" In the context of the apostle's previous letter, isn't it reasonable to conclude that Paul took for granted that his audience (the Thessalonians) would immediately recognize that statement as a connection to his teaching in 1 Thessalonians 4:13–18? If this is the meaning in context, the rapture (departing of believers from the earth) must occur *before* the other prophetic events of the day of Christ can unfold. Of course, once the Thessalonians received this correction, they could go forward without the fear of enduring the coming day of Christ. In fact, Paul previously taught them this truth in 1 Thessalonians 5:9.

The second possible translation is connected to the idea of a *metaphorical* departure. The King James translation in 1611 inexplicably changed the English rendering to the phrase "falling away first." We are all quite familiar with this rendering, but the tendency in our study is to view this phrase as a metaphorical falling away from the faith. Outside of the context of the two Thessalonian letters, the same Greek word translated "falling away" (*apostesia)* does refer to departing from the faith. But we should note the word is most often used to communicate the act of a person departing from another person or place.

The point is, as used in 2 Thessalonians 2:3, the word does not have to be thought of in terms of a departure from the faith. It can most certainly mean a *physical departure.* We should allow the greater context to settle the proper usage of the word in 2 Thessalonians 2:3. After all, it is the context that dictates how the translators render *apostesia* elsewhere in the New Testament. Consequently, it seems straightforward to conclude Paul is referring to the action of 1 Thessalonians 4:13–18 by use of the phrase "falling away first" or "departing first." Thus he is teaching that the event of 1 Thessalonians 4:13–18 *must* occur as a separate action distinct from the physical, visible return of Christ, which culminates the day of the Lord. The departure of the church and the appearance of the man of sin following the rapture *must* occur to set in motion the fulfillment of all the other prophecies related to the day of the Lord. Again, once the Thessalonians understood this, they could put their troubled minds to rest. They were not entering the tribulation period and would not be present when God pours out his wrath in that day!

If one is inclined to pursue the meaning of the phrase "falling away first" as a departure from the faith, then a problem arises. Apostasy is not something new to this church age. As a matter of fact, it characterizes the whole age! The spirit of antichrist has been in the world since the beginning of the church (cf. 1 Tim. 4:1; 1 John 2:18, 4:3; 2 John 7). In light of this fact, it seems most appropriate to allow the teaching of 1 Thessalonians 4:13–18 to drive the context in which we view the "departure or falling away" mentioned in 2 Thessalonians 2:3.

From this perspective, it is interesting to note that 2 Thessalonians 2:1–12 actually speaks of both phases of Christ's coming in one passage! Here it is:

- the rapture of the church (2:1, 3—our gathering unto him, departure)
- the man of sin revealed (2:3—seven-year tribulation begins)

- the man of sin desecrates the temple (2:4; Dan. 9:27)
- Christ destroys the man of sin (2:8)
- the day of the Lord culminates (2:8; Rev. 19:11–21)

Suggested Activities

Research the word *imminent* as it relates to the rapture (cf. Matt. 24:44 with 25:1–13).

Why should we view the return of Christ as our "blessed hope"?

Read Luke 21:36 and Revelation 3:10. What do these passages of Scripture indicate?

Regardless of the view one takes concerning the meaning of the phrase "*falling away first,*" the apostle Paul made it clear to the Thessalonians that two distinct, historic events *must* occur before the day of Christ can unfold. Not only will there be a falling away, but the man of sin must also be revealed. Paul also calls this individual the "son of perdition" (v. 3). These titles are referring to the appearance of the antichrist. The appearance of antichrist is a central theme of Bible prophecy. This man will be driven by Satan! While I do not believe it is appropriate to say the antichrist will be Satan incarnate (since *incarnate* is a term reserved only for the unique person of Christ), he most certainly will be possessed by Satan. In the person of the antichrist, Satan's rebellion against the rule of God will finally reach its full expression as he demands worship from the whole world (v. 4)!

This coming period of world history will be the most volatile spiritual time known to mankind. Multitudes of people will be deceived by the antichrist. Personally, I do not believe the world will refer to the man of sin as the antichrist. On the contrary, they will believe this man to be a great spiritual leader and a peace maker, not a deceiver. Those under the delusion of the antichrist will see him as "the truth." In fact, God will send them "strong delusion, that they should believe a lie: that they all might be damned who believed not the truth, but had pleasure in unrighteousness" (cf. vv. 11 and 12). Although most will be deceived, there will also be a great multitude that refuses to submit to the rule of the antichrist, and they will be persecuted unto the death (cf. Rev. 6:9–11, 7:9–17).

One of the interesting points of study that arises from verse 4 of this chapter is the prediction of a restored Jewish temple during this coming period of world history. The antichrist will desecrate this temple by entering it and demanding that the world worship him! This is the abomination of desolation Jesus confirmed in his reference to the book of Daniel (cf. Matt. 24:15; Dan. 8:9–13, 9:27). Currently there is no Jewish temple in Jerusalem. Consequently, the reconstruction of another temple must occur to provide the setting for fulfillment of this prophecy. Perhaps this will be a centerpiece of the covenant the antichrist establishes with Israel. This coming world dictator will certainly possess the political authority to bring such an event to fruition, in spite of objections from Israel's Muslim neighbors. Regardless, there will be a restored temple in Jerusalem. It is interesting to note that orthodox Jews in Israel are already making concrete plans to rebuild the temple as soon as it is politically feasible.

Another question arises in light of the fact that the antichrist will not promote the worship of the one true living God because he represents a false spirituality and will ultimately demand the worship of the world. *Why would he allow the Jews to build a temple that obviously will not honor him?* Even in a current state of unbelief, spiritual-minded Jews worship the Lord. Temple worship will seek to honor the God of Abraham, Moses, David, and the prophets. So, why allow it to be rebuilt?

I think the answer lies in the *progression* of things that will unfold. Remember, Satan transforms himself into an angel of light to appear to be something he is not! At first the antichrist will appear to be the world's "savior" as he brings in peace and seemingly resolves the problems troubling Israel and the world. But as his rule continues to unfold, Israel and the world will come to understand his real intentions. Israel will fully recognize the deceit of the antichrist when he desecrates the temple and demands that they worship him. It is exactly at this point in history that the "time of Jacob's trouble" will begin (cf. Jer. 30:7). Jesus gave very specific instructions to the Jews connected to this event and went on to say, "Then shall be great tribulation, such as was not since the beginning of the world to this time, no, nor ever shall be" (cf. Matt. 24:15–21). In light of these predictions, the rebuilding of the Jewish temple certainly has a prominent place in Bible prophecy.

In verse 5 of this chapter, Paul reminded the Thessalonians that he taught the truths of verses 3 and 4 when he was with them at the first. They should have recognized the spurious teachings of some who had troubled them with a radically different perspective on the coming of the Lord. The Thessalonians were not entering the immediate years that precede the "day of Christ." The great day of his wrath, which culminates in his visible return to earth, cannot take place until the "falling away" (the rapture of the church as detailed in 1 Thess. 4:13–18) and until the antichrist appears. Paul taught these things earlier, but now he was again seeking to establish the church in the right mind-set. Likewise, you and I need to keep this order in view to live with the "blessed hope" of his return at any moment.

Suggested Activities

Read the following passages for more teaching about the antichrist: Daniel 7–9, 11, Revelation 6:2; 13.

Note these points about the rise of the antichrist and his reign as a world dictator:

- It cannot occur until the church is removed (cf. 1 Thess. 5:9; 2 Thess. 2:7; Luke 21:36; Rev. 3:10).
- He rises to prominence within the revived Roman Empire (Dan. 9:26).
- According to Revelation 13:5, he will rule for forty-two months over the world, administering a one-world government, economy, and false religious system in relative peace (cf. 1 Thess. 5:1–3; Dan. 8:25).
- Satan gives him great power (Rev 13:2).
- He will negotiate a covenant with Israel and will establish peace between her and the nations around her (Dan. 9:27).
- He will break the covenant himself in the midst of the "week."
- He will desecrate the temple (a great warning sign of the time for Israel to flee to the mountains; cf. Matt. 24:16 and Rev.12:6, 14).
- He compels the world to worship him (cf. 2 Thess. 2:4; Rev. 13:5, 7:9–17).
- This action initiates the great tribulation spoken of by Jesus
- After the world sees his true colors, the temporary peace will turn to sudden destruction (Rev. 6:3–4; the red horse is released, bringing world war).
- The antichrist will be destroyed at the second coming and confined to the lake of fire (Rev. 19:20).

2 Thessalonians 2:6–12

> And now ye know what withholdeth that he might be revealed in his time. For the mystery of iniquity doth already work: only he who now letteth will let, until he be taken out of the way. And then shall that Wicked be revealed, whom the Lord shall consume with the spirit of his mouth, and shall destroy with the brightness of his coming: even him, whose coming is after the working of Satan with all power and signs and lying wonders, and with all deceivableness of unrighteousness in them that perish; because they received not the love of the truth, that they might be saved. And for this cause God shall send them strong delusion, that they should believe a lie: that they all might be damned who believed not the truth, but had pleasure in unrighteousness.

In verse 6, the apostle again compelled the Thessalonians to recall his earlier teaching when he was present with them. He said, "And now ye know what withholdeth (restrains or holds back) that he (antichrist) might be revealed in his time." Paul taught this church about the restraining influence of the Holy Spirit when he was present with them. That was why he said they knew or already understood why the antichrist could not come on the world scene. As the Thessalonians paused to reflect upon the earlier teaching from the apostle, these truths became clear again. In fact, the man of sin, the son of perdition, cannot be revealed until the restraining influence set forth in verses 6 and 7 is removed. Consequently, they were not approaching the day of Christ. They were not in the tribulation, nor were they approaching the great tribulation the Scripture clearly states is coming. Rather, they were to live with the understanding that the antichrist will be revealed in his time after the restrainer holding back his appearance is taken out of the way!

As we study verses 6 and 7 together, it should be clear that there is a definite restraining influence that prevents Satan from revealing his man of sin, the antichrist. These verses clearly indicate that he (the restrainer) must be removed before that wicked being will be revealed (v. 8). Who is this restrainer? Who has the power to prevent Satan from establishing a world order that will usher in the rule of the antichrist? The only reasonable answer is the Lord! Only a member of the Godhead can exercise such authority. A logical question follows: which member of the Triune Godhead currently manifests a worldwide influence sufficient to restrain Satan, and how does he do so? The answer is the Holy Spirit!

There is continuity in Paul's reasoning in this passage. Paul taught the Thessalonians to anticipate the rapture (1 Thess. 4:13–18). It is this world-shaking event that will remove the body of Christ from the earth and conclude the present ministry of the Holy Spirit through the church. Once the Holy Spirit's restraining influence through the church is removed at the rapture, then Satan will be free to reveal his man of sin, the ultimate lawless one. This line of reasoning provides strong support for a pretribulation rapture of the church. Remember, the Lord Jesus teaches us that he will not leave the church as an orphan. Rather, Jesus said he would come to us and abide with us forever. He has done so in the person of the Holy Spirit (cf. John 14:16–18). Thus, it is not possible for the Holy Spirit to be taken out of the way and the church to remain here! In fact, Paul is driving this home to the Thessalonians. This lesson follows for all subsequent believers: *We will not enter the tribulation and be present on the earth as the day of Christ unfolds; rather Christ will return for his bride and at the rapture remove the restraining influence of the Holy Spirit through the church, thus allowing Satan to reveal the antichrist and unleash unprecedented deception upon the world!*

Please take note of how deception will escalate under the rule of the antichrist (v. 9–10). Satan will unleash signs and lying wonders with such power that if it were possible, even the elect would be deceived (cf. Matt. 24:24–25)! Our world has never seen the full onslaught of Satan's power, but it is coming. Verse 10 goes on to show us why so many will be deceived. They did not receive the love of the truth so they might be saved. For this reason, God will send them a strong delusion so they will believe a lie and be condemned. Verse 11 should serve as a strong warning to anyone who is unwilling to acknowledge the truthfulness of God's Word. Progressively, those who are unwilling to acknowledge that God's Word is truth actually find pleasure in their choice to rebel against the rule of God. How wicked! In context, it seems quite appropriate that God will give them their desire and help them to follow that wicked one whom Jesus will destroy with the brightness of his coming.

Suggested Activities

Here are several questions to ponder connected to the rapture and the tribulation period:

1. Will those who hear the gospel and neglect to receive Christ prior to the rapture still have an opportunity to be saved?
2. In what way is the rapture a tremendous witness to the world of the truthfulness of God's Word? Why would the world proceed to ignore the implications of the rapture?
3. Immediately following the rapture of the church, the world will be left without a witness of the gospel. Who will preach the everlasting gospel during the rise and reign of the antichrist (cf. Rev. 14:6)?
4. If the church is raptured prior to the tribulation, who are the elect the Lord Jesus speaks of in Matthew 24:24? (Remember, this action occurs during the great tribulation., Matt. 24:21–24.)
5. What can we learn about the future work of the Holy Spirit following the rapture from Joel 2:28–32?

2 Thessalonians 2:13–17

> But we are bound to give thanks alway to God for you, brethren beloved of the Lord, because God hath from the beginning chosen you to salvation through sanctification of the Spirit and belief of the truth: whereunto he called you by our gospel, to the obtaining of the glory of our Lord Jesus Christ. Therefore, brethren, stand fast, and hold the traditions which ye have been taught, whether by word, or our epistle. Now our Lord Jesus Christ himself, and God, even our Father, which hath loved us, and hath given us everlasting consolation and good hope through grace, comfort your hearts, and stablish you in every good word and work.

Verses 13 and 14 are in perfect harmony with the lengthy teaching Paul would later give in the book of Romans concerning our salvation. Here he gives us a simple outline of salvation that includes the past, present, and future. First Paul says of the Thessalonians, "God has from the beginning chosen you to salvation." It is a most comforting thought to understand that God has chosen a people unto salvation. He did so in the eternal past before the foundation of the world. Salvation is not an afterthought with the living God. In his eternal counsels, the Lord chose a people unto himself. We gather from the study of Scripture that this choosing was based upon pure grace.

The Lord proceeded with the creation of all things with the full knowledge that the race would fall in Adam. However, God determined to deal with the entire race by extending an open invitation for all to accept his love and mercy in spite of the fact that all were undeserving. Thus God determined to lavish his grace upon those among the race who of their own volition returned love to him with a believing heart! It is in this context that God *chose* the Thessalonians to salvation. It should be pointed out that God does not arbitrarily choose some to salvation and some to damnation. Such behavior would not be consistent with his just nature. To choose some to salvation arbitrarily when the whole race is equally deserving of his condemnation would be partial and unjust. Therefore, God's chosen should be understood as those whom he foreknew would respond to his love.

Paul went on to say that the Thessalonians were chosen to salvation "through sanctification of the Spirit and belief of the truth." This is the present work of God in salvation. The Spirit of God sets apart believers in two ways. First, those who respond to the invitation of the Spirit to come to Christ and believe the truth are immediately sanctified or set apart to God in Christ. Second, the Spirit of God is present in the heart of a true believer and leads him or her into practical holiness. The believer is progressively set apart unto God by the leading of the Spirit. The result is godly, Christlike behavior as the believer puts away the old man and yields himself as a servant of righteousness.

Verse 14 goes on to speak of salvation as it relates to the future. The Thessalonians were called by the gospel "to the obtaining of the glory of our Lord Jesus Christ." The apostle John explained exactly what this means when he said, "Beloved, now are we the sons of God, and it doth not yet appear what we shall be: but we know that, when he shall appear, we shall be like him; for we shall see him as he is" (1 John 3:2). Our salvation includes our *glorification.* In that day, our bodies will put on incorruption and our redeemed humanity will be free from the presence of evil (sin)!

In light of such a glorious salvation, the apostle concluded his thought by saying, "Therefore, brethren, stand fast, and hold the traditions (teachings eventually fully capsulated in Holy Scripture) which you have been taught, whether by word, or our epistle." It is important to keep this statement in its historic context. At the time Paul wrote this epistle, the canon of Holy Scripture was not complete. It was certainly appropriate to admonish the church to follow the oral and written teachings of the apostles who were still alive. However, today we do not follow the traditions of any human teacher or organization. Rather, we judge all tradition in light of Holy Scripture. Any tradition that contradicts the authoritative, written Word of God must be rejected.

Paul ended this chapter with a prayer for the Thessalonians. His desire was that the Lord would comfort their hearts and establish them in every good word and work. This is exactly what the Lord desires for all of his people. The Lord will comfort us as we rest in his "everlasting consolation" and the "good hope" we possess "through grace." Praise the Lord!

Suggested Activities

Read Romans 8:28–38. Do you understand that a true believer is one of God's elect (chosen)? Can God lose one of his elect? Remember, God's written Word is designed to produce a full assurance of salvation in your heart (1 John 5:11–13). Do you recognize from this passage that as one of God's elect you will never perish? If so, you can rejoice with the full assurance that heaven is your home the moment after death!

As you study your Bible, take careful note of the phrase *in Christ*. This is an essential concept related to our salvation. A proper understanding of your *position* in Christ will lead to a wonderful, full assurance of salvation. The following verses are examples that contain the statement that we are "in Christ": Romans 8:1, 16:7; 2 Corinthians 5:17; Ephesians 2:6; 1 Peter 5:14.

Growth in personal holiness should be a serious concern for every disciple of Jesus Christ. Read the following passages for instruction that will "set you apart" unto the Lord as you conduct yourself in this world: Romans 12:2; Ephesians 5:1–21; Colossians 3:1–17; 1 Peter 1:13–22.

In light of the condition of our culture today, how should we specifically "stand fast" and hold to the truth of Scripture? Attempt to answer this question as you think of the following topics: *evolution, marriage, education, and spirituality.*

Can you cite an example of a tradition that contradicts Scripture? Are you willing to allow the Scripture to correct you should a personal tradition contradict Scripture?

CHAPTER 8

2 THESSALONIANS 3

2 Thessalonians 3:1–5

> Finally, brethren, pray for us, that the word of the Lord may have free course, and be glorified, even as it is with you: and that we may be delivered from unreasonable and wicked men: for all men have not faith. But the Lord is faithful, who shall stablish you, and keep you from evil. And we have confidence in the Lord touching you, that ye both do and will do the things which we command you. And the Lord direct your hearts into the love of God, and into the patient waiting for Christ.

As the apostle Paul approached the end of his second letter to the Thessalonians, he expressed a desire for their prayers. Paul desired the church to pray for him as he traveled onward teaching and preaching the gospel of the Lord Jesus Christ. He longed to see the word of the Lord touch others as it had impacted the Thessalonians. You will recall from 1 Thessalonians 2 that when these believers first heard Paul preach, they accepted his message as it was in truth, the Word of God and not merely the word of men (1 Thess. 2:13). The Word of God certainly had *free course* among the Thessalonians as they turned from idols to serve the only true God and his Son, the Lord Jesus Christ. Paul compelled the church to pray for similar success among others he would engage with the gospel.

It is essential for the Christian community to recognize the importance of prayer in the work of the Lord. Prayer must be behind our ministries if we are to be successful. This is a lesson we should not simply gloss over. Paul's desire for prayer is not an example of casual Christian conversation. Rather, it is an earnest plea for real prayer that can bring forth results! The work of the ministry, in which Paul was engaged, required earnest prayer. In light of this truth, all believers need to offer sincere prayer for their pastors and spiritual leaders. Like Paul, spiritual leaders often encounter "unreasonable and wicked men." As these leaders endeavor to advance the cause of Christ, they often experience great opposition inside and outside the church.

Paul cites a specific example of this in his words to the church at Corinth. He said to them, "If after the manner of men I have fought with beasts at Ephesus, what advantageth it me, if the dead rise not? let us eat and drink; for tomorrow we die" (1 Cor. 15:32). Note the descriptive words Paul used to refer to those men in Ephesus who opposed the advance of the gospel. He said he "fought with beasts" at Ephesus. Of course, he was not speaking of literal animals or of a literal battle. Instead he was referring to the opposition of those who were unwilling to accept the truth of the gospel.

Paul went on in 1 Corinthians 16 to say, "For a great door and effectual is opened unto me, and there are many adversaries" (1 Cor. 16:9). This is the reason he desired prayer. Not all men have faith or will accept *the faith*. Consequently, they argue against the gospel and seek to turn others away from the faith. Worse yet is the possibility that such unbelievers will seek to stop the preaching of the gospel by persecuting the messenger. Paul knew well what it was to experience opposition from adversaries in debate, legal skirmishes, and outright persecution. I am quite sure the apostle was very serious when he asked the Thessalonians to pray for him.

Like Paul, present-day pastors, evangelists, Bible teachers, and Christian ministries of all sorts are experiencing the same kind of opposition and need much prayer. Let us take to heart the need for fervent prayer on behalf of the spiritual leaders in our lives!

Paul moved on in verse 3 to express his great confidence in the Lord. He said, "But the Lord is faithful." Indeed, Paul experienced the Lord's faithfulness in his own life and believed the Lord would faithfully establish the Thessalonians and guard them against evil or "the evil one." He was also confident that the Thessalonians would continue to live in obedience to the commands he had set forth in person and in his first letter to them. Paul concluded this section with a twofold prayer for this church. First, he desired that their hearts would continually be directed into the love of God, and second, he desired that they would endure with courage the problems that will come as we wait for the Lord Jesus.

Suggested Activities

Do you engage in consistent prayer for your pastor? If not, will you commit to regular prayer on his behalf? If you do not have a pastor, will you make it a priority to find a church where you can actively serve the Lord and support the spiritual leadership with faithful attendance and prayer?

Read Ephesians 6:18–20. Did the apostle Paul also ask this church to pray for him, and if so, what did he hope their prayers would accomplish?

Paul felt confident that the Thessalonians would continue to obey the commands he gave the church. Read 1 Thessalonians 5 again, and list the commands you find in the chapter.

2 Thessalonians 3:6–18

> Now we command you, brethren, in the name of our Lord Jesus Christ, that ye withdraw yourselves from every brother that walketh disorderly, and not after the tradition which he received of us. For yourselves know how ye ought to follow us: for we behaved not ourselves disorderly among you; neither did we eat any man's bread for nought; but wrought with labour and travail night and day, that we might not be chargeable to any

> of you: not because we have not power, but to make ourselves an ensample unto you to follow us. For even when we were with you, this we commanded you, that if any would not work, neither should he eat. For we hear that there are some which walk among you disorderly, working not at all, but are busybodies. Now them that are such we command and exhort by our Lord Jesus Christ, that with quietness they work, and eat their own bread. But ye, brethren, be not weary in well doing. And if any man obey not our word by this epistle, note that man, and have no company with him, that he may be ashamed Yet count him not as an enemy, but admonish him as a brother. Now the Lord of peace himself give you peace always by all means. The Lord be with you all. The salutation of Paul with mine own hand, which is the token in every epistle: so I write. The grace of our Lord Jesus Christ be with you all. Amen.

In verse 6, the apostle Paul used very strong language in the original to set forth the authority he possessed as an apostle. He was dealing with a very real problem that occurred in Thessalonica that also troubles many local churches to this very day. Certain brothers (professed believers in the church) refused to obey the teaching (tradition) set forth by the apostle. Such behavior was "disorderly." In fact, it is always out of order to walk in deliberate disobedience to the commands of Holy Scripture! Today we possess the teaching of the apostles in the authoritative written Word of God. We are to obey it! Particularly, here we are commanded in the name of the Lord Jesus Christ to withdraw from professed believers who refuse to work and are busybodies!

This instruction does not mean we should jump to hasty conclusions in relationship to fellow believers. Paul was not talking about separating from brothers over disagreements related to nonessential doctrines. However, he did expect believers to *live responsibly*! Any fanaticism that leads believers to live irresponsibly is not acceptable. Under such circumstances, it may be necessary to withdraw fellowship from that brother until he is willing to accept correction.

At the heart of Paul's discussion in these verses is the problem of believers who refuse to work! Paul left no such example! As a matter of fact, he gave up the privilege of support from this church to compel them to work as he did! In so doing, Paul went the second mile to compel all members of the church to live responsibly by engaging in productive work. In so doing, they would eat their own bread with quietness. Instead of being busybodies (idle gossips meddling in the business of others), they were to be hard workers in honest professions (cf. Titus 3:14). Again, if any refused to obey this command, the rest of the church was to have no company with them for the purpose of admonition (cf. 3:14–15).

As the apostle closed this letter, he encouraged the church to "be not weary in well-doing." Never stop doing good! This is a simple statement from the Holy Spirit that can guide us daily. Look for opportunities to do good. Make it your business to bless others by following through with acts of kindness that meet real needs. Do good in the Spirit of Christ!

Paul concluded his letter with a gracious benediction and gave the salutation with his own hand. Of course, the Thessalonians could certainly compare other supposed letters from Paul by looking for his unique salutation. Any supposed letter from the apostle that lacked his personal salutation did not contain teaching from the apostle (cf. 2 Thess. 2:2).

May the grace of our Lord Jesus Christ be with you.

Suggested Activities

Besides the problem of neglecting honest work if one is able, how might believers in a local church conduct themselves "disorderly"?

In what ways should the promise of Christ's return motivate believers? Should the promise of our Lord's return ever be misconstrued as an excuse for irresponsible behavior (cf. Luke 19:11–27)?

The Word of God certainly sets forth a strong work ethic. Read the following passages, and evaluate your own attitude toward work in general: Proverbs 24:27, 31:27, 13:4, 20:4, 26:16, 18:9, 26:14, 20:13, 24:30–34, 6:6–11; 1 Timothy 5:8; Ephesians 6:5–8.

ADDENDUM

COMFORT ONE ANOTHER

One of the necessary roles of a pastor is to function as a source of comfort when individuals or families face the loss of someone dear to them. Death under any set of circumstances brings sorrow of heart and a general desire on the part of the bereaved for comfort. Real comfort at such times of loss is rooted in a clear understanding of the Word of God. The Word of God guides us into a proper understanding of how death originated. Furthermore, it explains exactly what happens to an individual at the moment of death and answers common questions like, "Can we meet our loved ones again, will there be a resurrection, and will death ever be abolished?"

As a pastor, I have dealt with these and other questions related to death on numerous occasions in an attempt to provide comfort to those enduring a difficult season of loss. I would like to submit to my readers the following devotional thoughts gleaned from my years as a pastor in an effort to provide a source of comfort for those working through the emotional burden associated with the death of a loved one or a close friend.

Understanding the Big Picture

The most difficult aspect of grieving is often related to the question "*why*?" Why did my mom or dad have to die now? Why did this dear loved one die under these circumstances? Why did my child have to die? Why was this friend's life cut so short? I think it is quite natural for us to ask such questions as we grieve. In some way, this is part of the grieving process. However, I believe it is important for all of us to see the big picture answer to the question "why?" It is important for you to understand that there was a time at the beginning of the creation when death *did not* exist! The original very good creation detailed in God's inspired Word did not include death! At the end of the creation week, God pronounced everything good (Gen. 1:31). It was not until *after* the first man, Adam, disobeyed God that death entered into the world (Gen. 2:15–17, Rom. 5:12). The reason our world is filled with death is directly connected to the fact that we live in a fallen world. By one man sin entered into the world and death by sin. Death has now passed upon all men, for all have sinned!

Although there are certainly many ways one can leave this life, we must keep this big-picture truth in view. Regardless of how it comes or when it comes, death has now passed upon all men because of sin. Death is now an enemy to all of us (1 Cor. 15:26). In fact, death is *near* us at all times! Our brief lives upon this earth are described as a vapor that appears for just a little while (James 4:14). The patriarch Job spoke to this reality in the following words: "Man that is born of woman is of few days, and full of trouble. He cometh forth like a flower, and is cut down: he fleeth also as a shadow, and continueth not" (Job 14:1–2). We would be wise to pray as King David did when he said, "Lord, make me to know mine end, and the measure of my days, what it is; that I may know how frail I am" (Ps. 39:4). Indeed, life is frailer than we generally acknowledge, and in a certain sense, there is but a step between each of us and death!

Have you come to grips with this scriptural truth? Ultimately we all die, whether young or old, tragically or peacefully, because sin brought death into God's original very good creation. An understanding of this basic truth will free you from the temptation to blame God for the death of someone dear. In fact, it was mankind's sin that introduced death into the world. Thankfully, God has provided hope for all men through the gift of his Son, the Lord Jesus Christ. You see, through his great sacrifice upon the cross, the Lord Jesus destroyed him who had the power of death, that is, the Devil (Heb. 2:14–15). Furthermore, the Lord Jesus delivers us from the bondage of the fear of death by virtue of our faith in him! We understand that Christ has actually abolished death, and consequently in the resurrection we will share in his victory! Praise the Lord! God has promised a coming day when death will be destroyed once and for all!

The Word of God declares:

> And I saw a new heaven and a new earth: for the first heaven and the first earth were passed away … And God shall wipe away all tears from their eyes; and there shall be no more death, neither sorrow, nor crying, neither shall there be any more pain: for the former things are passed away. And he that sat upon the throne said, Behold, I make all things new. And he said unto me, Write: for these words are true and faithful. (Rev. 21:1, 4–5)

While we must commit the various circumstances surrounding death into the hands of a sovereign God, we can find great comfort in knowing that God has made future provision to wipe away all the sorrow caused by sin and death when he makes all things new!

The Christian Perspective on Death

For many facing a season of loss, death causes great uncertainty. But such a state of mind can be calmed if one knows the Holy Scriptures. Sir Walter Scott, when dying, told his servant to bring the Book, to which the servant replied, "Which book, sir?" Sir Walter answered, "When a man is dying, there is only one Book—bring the Bible!" My dear friend, there is only one book in the whole world that can give true peace of mind as one faces the prospect of dying.

The Bible makes it abundantly clear that man is created in the image of God. One of the ways we reflect the image of the eternal God lies in the fact that we exist as eternal souls. While there was a time when you and I did not exist, there will never be a time in the future when we cease to exist! We are now creatures of eternity and reflect God's image in that regard. This is an awesome truth to come to grips with. The fact is, we will spend eternity somewhere.

The moment of physical death is defined in the Bible as the departure of the human soul/spirit from the body (Gen. 35:18; Eccles.12:6–7; James 2:26). This transition into the immaterial world does not have to be an experience filled with fear and dread. In fact, the Christian perspective on death has the power to fill the heart of a dying man with a calm assurance and a certainty unknown by those of other religious persuasions. But just how and where does this confidence come from?

In the gospel of St. John, the Lord Jesus Christ told a grieving woman by the name of Martha that her departed brother would rise again. Martha in reply told Jesus, "I know that he shall rise again in the resurrection at the last day." Jesus replied with a declaration that has the power to give assurance to anyone willing to believe upon him. He said, "I am the resurrection, and the life: he that believeth in me, though he were dead, yet shall he live: And whosoever liveth and believeth in me shall never die. Believest thou this?" Martha proceeded to confess her personal faith in the Lord Jesus by saying, "Yea, Lord: I believe that thou art the Christ, the Son of God, which should come into the world" (John 11:23–27).

Confidence to face the moment of death without fear comes from a personal relationship to the Lord Jesus Christ. He alone has the words of eternal life (John 6:68). Those who trust Christ as their personal Savior receive the free gift of eternal life. Those who understand they possess eternal life face death with a settled *inner knowing* that "to depart and be with Christ is far better" (Phil. 1:23).

Believers with this kind of confidence know the promises of Christ and are fully persuaded that *nothing*, including death, can separate them from the love of God that is in Christ Jesus (Rom. 8:38–39)! Consequently, to die simply means to be absent from the body and immediately present with the Lord (2 Cor. 5:8). But death must finally be swallowed up in victory at the return of Christ when believers receive a resurrected, glorified body. Just as the moment of physical death *unclothed* the believer as the soul departed into the presence of Christ, the moment of Christ's return will *clothe* the believer in an incorruptible, immortal body (cf. 1 Thess. 4:13–18; 1 Cor. 15:35–57; 2 Cor. 5:1–8). The future physical resurrection of every believer *redeems* the body and completes the final aspect of salvation as death is swallowed up in victory (Rom. 8:23)!

Perhaps as you read these words, these truths are becoming real to you for the first time. May I ask you some very personal questions? Do you believe that Jesus is the Christ, the Son of God who came for your salvation? Do you accept his death on the cross as the full payment for all your sin? Do you believe that God raised Jesus from the dead? Will you right now bow your head and confess to God your need of Jesus Christ as Savior? Will you ask him to come into your heart and save you? If you have never called upon the Lord and personally placed your faith in the Lord Jesus Christ as your only hope of heaven, will you do it now? *I trust that you can see from Holy Scripture that receiving Christ into your heart by faith is the only way to be prepared for death.* If you desire to make a personal commitment to Jesus Christ, please take the time to pray this prayer and mean it from your heart:

> Dear Lord, I know I am a sinner with no hope of heaven. But I believe Jesus is the Christ, the Son of God who died on the cross to satisfy the divine wrath against my sin. I believe he arose from the dead and now lives to secure my salvation at your right hand. I do now trust Jesus as my Savior. I invite him to come into my heart, and I ask you to save me for Jesus' sake. Thank you for loving me! Thank you for forgiving me! Thank you for saving me! Thank you for giving me eternal life! I love you, Lord Jesus, and pray now that you will lead me and guide me by your Spirit, whom I now receive into my heart. Father, this prayer I offer in the name of your Son the Lord Jesus Christ. Amen.

My friend, I can tell you on the authority of God's Word that if you just opened your heart to the Lord Jesus by praying that prayer, you are saved! (Read Acts 16:31; Rom. 10:9–13; John 3:15–17.)

Quotes From Christians As They Departed This Life

There is a stark contrast between the death of a Christian and those who do not know the Lord. Someone has said, "I have never known anyone who on his deathbed repented of being a Christian!" Indeed! Christians die well! Listed below are quotes from some well-known Christians as they went to be with the Lord. The convictions expressed in these quotes summarize the confidence that multitudes of believers have enjoyed as the day of death overtook them.

Lady Powerscourt (1800)—"One needs a great many Scriptures to live by, but the only Scripture that a person needs to die by is 1 John 1:7; and that verse never was sweeter to me than at this moment."

William Wilberforce (1833)—"My affections are so much in Heaven that I can leave you all without a regret; yet I do not love you less, but God more."

Polycarp (AD 155)—Christian martyr and disciple of John: "Eighty and six years have I served Him, and He has done me nothing but good. How could I curse Him, my Lord and Saviour?"

Philip Melanchthon (1560)—When several portions of Scripture had been read to him, he was asked by his son-in-law if he would have anything else, and his reply was in these emphatic words: "Nothing else but heaven!"

Samuel Rutherford (1615)—"Mine eyes shall see my Redeemer. He has pardoned, loved, washed me and given me joy unspeakable and full of glory. I feed on manna. Glory, glory, glory to my Creator and Redeemer forever! Glory, glory shines in Immanuel's land!"

John Bunyan (1688)—author of *The Pilgrim's Progress:* "Weep not for me, but yourselves. I go to the Father of our Lord Jesus Christ who will, through the mediation of His blessed Son, receive me, though a sinner, where I hope we shall meet to sing the new song and remain everlastingly happy, world without end."

David Brainerd (1747)—well-known missionary: "I am going into eternity, and it is sweet to me to think of eternity; the endlessness of it makes it sweet. But, oh! what shall I say of the eternity of the wicked? I cannot mention it nor think of it; the thought is too dreadful!"

Michael Faraday (1867)—chemist, electrician, and philosopher. A distinguished scientist, calling on him, put to him this question: "Have you conceived to yourself what will be your occupation in the next world?" Hesitating awhile, Faraday answered, "Eye hath not seen, nor ear heard, neither have entered into the heart of man, the things which God hath prepared for them that love him." And then he added, in his own words, "I shall be with Christ, and that is enough."

Brownlow North (1875)—profligate nobleman who became a preacher, said, "The blood of Jesus Christ his Son cleanseth us from all sin—that is the verse on which I am now dying. One wants no more."

Earl Cairns (1885)—Lord High Chancellor of England: "God loves me and cares for me. He has pardoned all my sins for Christ's sake, and I look forward to the future with no dread."

Sidney Cooper (1902)—Royal Academician, wrote when ninety-eight: "I have full faith in Thy atonement, and I am confident of Thy help. The precious blood I fully rely on. Thou art the source of my comfort. I have no other. I want no other."

John Pierpont Morgan (1913)—American millionaire, first paragraph of his will: "I commit my soul into the hands of my Saviour, in full confidence that having redeemed it and washed it in His most precious blood, He will present it faultless before the throne of my Heavenly Father. I entreat my children to maintain and defend at all hazards and at any cost of personal sacrifice the blessed doctrine of the complete atonement for sin through the blood of Jesus Christ, once offered, and through that alone."

Augustus Toplady (1778)—author of *Rock of Ages*: "The consolations of God to such an unworthy wretch are so abundant that He leaves me nothing to pray for but a continuance of them. I enjoy Heaven already in my soul."

Benjamin Abbott (1796)—"Glory to God! I see Heaven sweetly opened before me!"

Dwight L. Moody (1899)—"Earth recedes; Heaven opens before me. No, this is no dream, Will. It is beautiful. It is like a trance. If this is death, it is sweet. There is no valley here. God is calling me, and I must go."

Sir David Brewster (1868)—inventor of the kaleidoscope: "I will see Jesus: I shall see Him as He is. I have had the light for many years. Oh, how bright it is! I feel so safe and satisfied!"

Matthew Henry (1714)—famous Bible commentator: "You have been used to take notice of the sayings of dying men—this is mine ... that a life spent in the service of God and communion with Him is the most pleasant life that anyone can live in this world."

Paul the apostle (AD 66)—"I have fought a good fight, I have finished my course, I have kept the faith: Henceforth there is laid up for me a crown of righteousness."

Consider now the contrast of another Christian as he died with that of a famous leader of a different spirituality.

Sankey or Gandhi!
(Two Views of Life, Two Different Ends)

Ira D. Sankey (famed song leader for D. L. Moody) lived in Brooklyn the last few years of his life, and after years of blindness, he died there in 1908. When a cousin visited him in Brooklyn in May 1907, out of his blindness and frailty, Sankey dictated a farewell message to his friends:

> I believe in Him who said, "Verily, verily, I say unto you, He that believeth on me hath everlasting life" (John 6:47).
>
> I believe in the Son of God with all my soul, might, mind and strength and am, therefore, saved by the Word of One who cannot lie. I have only a little longer weary tossing on the billows' foam, only a little longer of earthly darkness, and then the sunshine of the Father's throne. So sure am I of meeting in Heaven those of my friends who are following the Lamb that I send them this final message that God is love. Good night; good night.
>
> (Signed) Ira D. Sankey

The contrasting view is the one held by the famous Indian Ghandi. Some so-called Christian leaders have tried to represent Ghandi as a Christian because of his pacifism and personal standards of morality. But those who designate Ghandi as a Christian need to remember his own words:

> I must tell you in all humility that Hinduism, as I know it, entirely satisfies my soul, fills my whole being, and I find solace in the Bhagavad and Upanishads.

Here is the special quotation we wish to mention. Shortly before his death, according to the press, Ghandi said:

> My days are numbered. I am not likely to live very long—perhaps a year or a little more. For the first time in fifty years, I find myself in the slough of despond. All about me is darkness; I am praying for light.

Sankey's eyes were blind, but the light of the presence of Christ was flooding his soul. Ghandi had his eyes; but, alas, rejecting Christ, he had left his soul in darkness.

The Comfort of a Personal Testimony

Let me relate to you the testimony of a dear brother in the Lord who left his family with an amazing, unexplainable expression. Brother Dean was a dear member of our congregation a number of years ago. He loved the Lord, and I enjoyed his fellowship and appreciated his faithfulness to the house of God. Through the years, Dean's heart was weakened by a number of heart attacks until finally another attack placed him in the hospital and this time in a coma.

He lay in the bed without any expression on his face and absolutely no communication with his family in any way. He simply lay there, obviously near the point of death as a result of all the complications related to this latest heart attack. After three days or so of being in this condition, without any warning, a beautiful, full smile graced his face, and he took his final breath. Those by his bedside saw this sweet smile and the expression of joy it communicated without a single word spoken and with his eyes fully shut.

That smile spoke volumes! While his physical eyes were closed to the world he left behind, his departing soul lit up his face with an absolutely unexplainable smile that left no doubt in the minds of his loved ones that heaven was now in plain view! Think about it! Absolutely no facial expression of any kind, no communication of any kind, and no movement of any kind for over three days—but suddenly a facial expression with a smile so radiant that it left a sense of awe and wonder about the glory he entered as his soul departed the body! Indeed, Christians do die well!

Dr. John R. Rice Learns about How to Die

The late Dr. John Rice, founder of the Sword of the Lord and a fruitful evangelist for many years, shared this heart-touching testimony of his own dear mother, whom he saw pass into eternity when he was just a five-year-old boy. In many ways this testimony tells the story of a great many believers who in similar fashion crossed the river we call death. Let this story comfort and bless your heart.

Dr. Rice wrote:

> I stood by the grave of my mother and looked down at that sandy mound in a country cemetery and lifted my heart to God in thanksgiving that the grave was already conquered. That grave was only a quiet bed where sleeps for a little time the body of my dear mother. But when Christ comes back for His own, my mother will come too and receive her glorified body, raised from the dead.
>
> Once I drew back with horror from death, but I have learned that death to the Christian is not crossing chilly waters, is not facing a fearsome monster, is not the grip of a cold hand on the throat or an icy breath in the face. Death for the child of God is simply sweet release from care and sorrow, the end of sin and disappointment, and the entering into the sweet presence of Christ!
>
> "For to me to live is Christ, and to die is gain" (Phil. 1:21). To die is gain. "Having a desire to depart, and to be with Christ; which is far better" (v. 23)! Death already has his teeth pulled as far as the saint is concerned. Christ, who died for sinners, rising again from the dead for our justification, ascending on high

ever to live as our High Priest, has taken away the sting of death.

In a country home near Red River in Texas, my mother lay dying. We children were called from our play, and we did not understand why everybody wept but Mother. Mother lay on her bed and talked about Christ and Heaven. She said, "Will you sing and play for me, Georgia!"

And Cousin Georgia answered, "What shall I sing, Aunt Sadie?" My mother said, "Sing

How firm a foundation,
Ye saints of the Lord,
Is laid for your faith
In his excellent Word."

So Cousin Georgia went to the little cottage organ and played and sang with trembling voice those blessed words. And my mother rejoiced and praised God while she sang.

Then one by one we were called to promise that we would meet Mother in Heaven, and promise we did. I was only five years old, and yet I remember that scene—how we stood about the room and looked on: grieving husband, four little children and kinspeople. Then my mother looked up, up, up with a glad smile and said, "I can see Jesus and my baby now!"

So she closed her eyes and went to sleep, and we knew that she was with Jesus and the little one who had gone to Him just a few months before.

> Thank God, I learned in my childhood how a Christian can die, and I am not afraid of death. Thank God, the Lord Jesus Christ has taken the sting out of death! The only way, then, to have peace about death is to have Christ as your Saviour. I beg you to trust Him today with all your heart.[2]

I Shall Go to Him, but He Shall Not Return to Me

Without question, one of the most difficult things to experience is the loss of a child. King David sought the Lord for the healing of his infant child born out of his adulterous relationship with Bathsheba (2 Sam. 12:15–23). However, David's prayer and fasting could not prevail, and the child died. Upon hearing this news, King David gathered himself, washed and changed his clothes, and then proceeded to go up to the house of the Lord, where he worshipped. Afterward he returned to his own house and sat down for a meal.

Those around the king were surprised that he could pick himself up and move forward without additional grieving. David then explained that while the child lived, he sought for God's mercy, but now that the child was gone, he fully understood that he could not bring the child back regardless of how he might grieve. Rather than becoming excessively distraught, David embraced the assurance that one day

---

2 John Rice, *When Skeletons Come Out of Their Closets*. Sword of the Lord, Murfreesboro, TN.

he would see his child again! What a comfort it is to dwell upon this coming reality. Personal faith in the Savior brings the assurance that you will meet that little one again. What a joy it will be on that day!

Sadly, I have stood with a number of families over the years as they said good-bye to an infant child. Such loss produces a different kind of grieving that is known only to the hearts of the parents involved. With that in mind, I composed the following poem in memory of one of those little ones. I submit it here with the hope that it might be a comfort to others who have known similar sorrow.

Sweet Little Baby Boy

Sweet little baby boy
You fill our thoughts today
We wonder if you know
What words could never say

How we wish we could have known
The joy of watching you grow
How we wish we could have shown
The love you were meant to know

But God who formed you in the womb
Planned a different path
His purpose was to call you home
Where we all will meet at last

You're now another treasure
Where saints and angels trod
Heaven is yours, I'm sure
For of such is the kingdom of God

So we look away by faith
To a time of endless joy
When Jesus the Resurrection wakes
Our sweet little baby boy

Pastor Rusty Yost
4/14/97

Resurrection! Could there be a more precious word in a fallen world? Death is an intruder into God's very good creation. It has wreaked untold sorrow upon the human heart and would leave us utterly in despair except for its antidote. What is our light in the darkness? My friend, it is the word *resurrection!* Is there an answer to death? Is there a victory that can be worked against this greatest of enemies? Our Lord boldly declares, "I am the resurrection and the life!" Jesus is the conquering seed of the woman sent forth of his Father to banish this enemy and restore all things! What victory! What hope we have in Christ! Not only will our little ones live again, but all those who know and trust the Lord Jesus Christ will live again with immortal, incorruptible bodies when Jesus, the Resurrection, returns again!

Devotional Thoughts on Sudden, Unexpected Death

The Scripture says, "To everything there is a season, and a time to every purpose under heaven: a time to be born, and a time to die" (Eccles. 3:1–2a). In Psalm 31 we also read, "But I trusted in thee, O Lord: I said, Thou art my God. My times are in thy hand" (Psalm 31:14–15a). While no one doubts that the time of our birth is in the Lord's hand, it is sometimes overlooked that the time of our death is as well. Our times are in his hand—the time of our birth *and* the time of our death. If a sparrow cannot fall to the ground without the notice of our heavenly Father, it is most certain that we cannot leave this walk of life without the hand of our heavenly Father is in it. What may seem accidental and tragic from our perspective must be committed to the Lord who alone ultimately rules over such circumstances.

We are brought then to the necessity of absolute trust in our heavenly Father, who works all things after the counsel of His own will. Consider with me for a moment the amazing account in the Old Testament of a man named Enoch. The Bible says Enoch walked with God. No doubt Enoch enjoyed his family. He was a man of godly character. He had a testimony in his community. People knew Enoch walked with God. And one day Enoch did not come home. The Bible makes this statement about the unique circumstances surrounding Enoch's departure from this life: "And Enoch walked with God: and he was not; for God took him."

While it is true that Enoch did not experience physical death as we know it, nonetheless the effect on his family would have been the same. They experienced both the sorrow of separation from Enoch along with the joy of knowing he was with the Lord. But please take note of the fact that "*God took him.*"

Can anything less be said about a child of God, whether his or her departure is somewhat expected or totally unexpected? Sometimes individuals carry a great burden because they see themselves as the reason someone died. But that thought must be tempered with an understanding that for reasons we do not fully grasp, God "took him." If you are dealing with the grief of mind that your actions caused an accidental death, please cast that burden upon the Lord! It is a weight no one can bear up under. Whether death comes naturally or whether it comes tragically, it belongs in the hands of almighty God!

Jesus Wept!

One of the most interesting stories from the life of Jesus Christ as recorded in the Word of God is found in John 11. In that chapter we find Jesus in the home of a grieving family who had lost a dear loved one to death. Their hearts were broken, and as Jesus stood by them, he was deeply moved himself. In fact, the Bible says that Jesus wept as a result.

If you are grieving the loss of someone dear it is

comforting to understand that the Son of God has stood where you are today. He knows what it is to grieve the loss of someone close to the heart. And he invites you to come to him. Jesus says, "Come unto me, all you that labour and are heavy laden, and I will give you rest. Take my yoke upon you, and learn of me; for I am meek and lowly in heart: and you shall find rest unto your souls. For my yoke is easy, and my burden is light" (Matt. 11:28–30). Come to Christ today with your tears. He knows and understands and will comfort you as no human source can.

The Lord Jesus Has a Deep Desire for His Own!

You will recall that the apostle Paul said to depart this life and "to be with Christ" is far better! It is the Lord's will that each of his redeemed be with him where he is. In John's gospel we read, "Father, I will that they also, whom thou hast given me, be with me where I am; that they may behold my glory, which thou hast given me: for thou lovedst me before the foundation of the world" (John 17:24). The Lord Jesus is praying to the Father in this passage. Please take careful note of Jesus' desire for his people to be where he is! My dear friend, Christ longs for the day when all his redeemed will finally be home in his presence. Furthermore, it is our Lord's will that we behold his glory! And we shall behold him!

What a comfort it is to understand that our departed loved ones who died with their trust in Christ are even now beholding his glory. Their eyes have seen the King in all of his beauty! The land once far off is now their homeland! They are *with* the Lord!

To Be with Christ Is Far Better!

How is it far better? Well, consider these wonderful thoughts.

First, it is far better because in his presence is the fullness of joy.

Next, in his presence is perfect peace. There is never a storm cloud in God's heaven.

Next, in his presence is perfect liberty. Where the Spirit of the Lord is, there is liberty. We will experience this blessing without measure in heaven. In his presence, there is freedom from all fear, all anxiety, and all worry.

Next, in his presence there is perfect security. There will be no evil in God's heaven. There will never be anything of any sort to disturb the tranquility of heaven.

Next, in his presence there is no lack of any kind. All the human soul, spirit, and body needs will be supplied in eternal ages to come by our faithful Creator and Redeemer.

Finally, it is far better because we trade our afflictions here for the glory there!

In Search of a City

In Hebrews 11, we find a discussion concerning the exploits of some of the Old Testament saints. Abraham is on this list. The Scripture says of Abraham:

> By faith Abraham, when he was called to go out into a place which he should after receive for an inheritance, obeyed; and he went out not knowing whither he went. By faith he sojourned in the land of promise, as in a strange country, dwelling in tabernacles with Isaac and Jacob, the heirs with him of the same promise: For he looked for a city which hath foundations, whose builder and maker is God.

When Abraham left Ur of the Chaldees, his mind was not simply on a new homeland in this temporal life. Rather, he had engaged in a journey of faith in search of a city whose builder and maker is God. Deep in Abraham's heart lived desires for something more than the temporal blessings of this life. This is the common testimony of all those who have embraced the call of God. Like the saints of old, we confess that we are strangers and pilgrims on the earth. We seek a country, a better country—that is, a heavenly country. Like the saints of old, God is not ashamed to be called our God, for he has prepared for us a city!

It is a city whose foundations are as eternal as the throne of God itself. This city will never need a hospital, a nursing home, or an extended care facility. It is a city where no one ever grows old and death is not permitted to enter. It is a city where no sad farewells are ever spoken and night can never come. It is a city where no evil can trouble the human heart. There will never be a broken heart there. It is a city where the soul is forever contented, and sighing and weeping will have faded, to be remembered no more. It is a city where all is the expression of the heart of a loving Redeemer who has gone to prepare a place for us. It is a city full of the glory of God and eternal joy that flows from the riches of his grace lavished upon his redeemed. Oh, what a city! In light of our salvation and what God has prepared for those who love him, death need not be feared at all. In fact, we set our affection there in a greater way with each passing day, and as our spiritual sight grows, there is a deepening desire to depart and be with Christ, which is far better.

Comfort One Another with These Words

In 1 Thessalonians 4:18 we read, "Wherefore comfort one another with these words." This statement is in the context of the apostle's teaching on the return of Christ found in the preceding verses. When Christ returns, he will bring our departed loved ones with him, they will receive resurrected bodies, and we will likewise be changed to meet them and the Lord in the air! What comfort these great truths bring to the heart!

As with this passage in 1 Thessalonians, there are many other verses of Holy Scripture that comfort us by bringing a proper understanding of death and the promise of eternal life into view. Below I have compiled a selection of passages that I trust will minister to your heart. While we certainly struggle with seasons of sorrow as a result of death, God's Word brings comfort and assurance lest we "sorrow without hope." I pray the Word of God will fill you with great peace as you mediate upon its unchanging promises.

> This is my comfort in my affliction: for thy word hath quickened me. (Ps. 119:50)
>
> Blessed are they that mourn: for they shall be comforted. (Matt. 5:4)
>
> I will not leave you comfortless: I will come to you. (John 14:18)
>
> For whatsoever things were written aforetime were written for our learning, that we through patience and comfort of the scriptures might have hope. (Rom. 15:4)
>
> Blessed be God, even the Father of our Lord Jesus Christ, the Father of mercies, and the God of all comfort; who comforteth us in all our tribulation, that we may be able to comfort them which are in any

trouble, by the comfort wherewith we ourselves are comforted of God. (2 Cor. 1:3–4)

Nevertheless God, that comforteth those that are cast down, comforted us by the coming of Titus. (2 Cor. 7:6)

But now is Christ risen from the dead, and become the firstfruits of them that slept. For since by man came death, by man came also the resurrection of the dead. For as in Adam all die, even so in Christ shall all be made alive. But every man in his own order: Christ the firstfruits; afterward they that are Christ's at his coming. Then cometh the end, when he shall have delivered up the kingdom to God, even the Father; when he shall have put down all rule and all authority and power. For he must reign, till he hath put all enemies under his feet. The last enemy that shall be destroyed is death. (1 Cor. 15:20–26)

So also is the resurrection of the dead. It is sown in corruption; it is raised in incorruption: it is sown in dishonour; it is raised in glory: it is sown in weakness; it is raised in power: it is sown a natural body; it is raised a spiritual body. There is a natural body, and there is a spiritual body. And so it is written, The first man Adam was made a living soul; the last Adam was made a quickening spirit. Howbeit that was not first which is spiritual, but that which is natural; and afterward that which is spiritual. The first man is of the earth, earthy: the second man is the Lord from heaven. As is the earthy, such are they also that are earthy: and as is the heavenly, such are they also that are heavenly. And as we have borne the image of the earthy, we shall also bear the image of the heavenly. Now this I say, brethren, that flesh and blood cannot inherit the kingdom of God; neither doth corruption inherit incorruption. Behold, I shew you a mystery; We shall not all sleep, but we shall all be changed, in a moment, in the twinkling of an eye, at the last trump: for the trumpet shall sound, and the dead shall be raised incorruptible, and we shall be changed. For this corruptible must put on incorruption, and this mortal must put on immortality. So when this corruptible shall have put on incorruption, and this mortal shall have put on immortality, then shall be brought to pass the saying that is written, Death is swallowed up in victory. O death, where is thy sting? O grave, where is thy victory? The sting of death is sin; and the strength of sin is the law. But thanks be to God, which giveth us the victory through our Lord Jesus Christ. (1 Cor. 15:42–57)

But I would not have you to be ignorant, brethren, concerning them which are asleep, that ye sorrow not, even as others which have no hope. For if we believe that Jesus died and rose again, even so them also which sleep in Jesus will God bring with him. For this we say unto you by the word of the Lord, that we which are alive and remain unto the coming of the Lord shall not prevent them which are asleep. For the Lord himself shall descend from heaven with a shout, with the voice of the archangel, and with the trump of God: and the dead in Christ shall rise first: then we which are alive and remain shall be caught up together with them in the clouds, to meet the Lord in the air: and so shall we ever be with the Lord. Wherefore comfort one another with these words. (1 Thess. 4:13–18)

For we know that if our earthly house of this tabernacle were dissolved, we have a building of God, an house not made with hands, eternal in the heavens. For in this we groan, earnestly desiring to be clothed upon with our house which is from heaven: if so be that being clothed we shall not be found naked. For we that are in this tabernacle do groan, being burdened: not for that we would be unclothed, but clothed upon, that mortality might be swallowed up of life. Now he that hath wrought us for the selfsame thing is God, who also hath given unto us the earnest of the Spirit. Therefore we are always confident, knowing that, whilst we are at home in the body, we are absent from the Lord: (for we walk by faith, not by sight:) we are confident, I say, and willing rather to be absent from the body, and to be present with the Lord. (2 Cor. 5:1–8)

For to me to live is Christ, and to die is gain. But if I live in the flesh, this is the fruit of my labour: yet what I shall choose I wot not. For I am in a strait betwixt two, having a desire to depart, and to be with Christ; which is far better. (Phil. 1:21–23)

Now a certain man was sick, named Lazarus, of Bethany, the town of Mary and her sister Martha. (It was that Mary which anointed the Lord with ointment, and wiped his feet with her hair, whose brother Lazarus was sick.) Therefore his sisters sent unto him, saying, Lord, behold, he whom thou lovest is sick. When Jesus heard that, he said, This sickness is not unto death, but for the glory of God, that the Son of God might be glorified thereby. Now Jesus loved Martha, and her sister, and Lazarus. When he had heard therefore that he was sick, he abode two days still in the same place where he was. Then after that saith he to his disciples, Let us go into Judaea again. His disciples say unto him, Master, the Jews of late sought to stone thee; and goest thou thither again? Jesus answered, Are there not twelve hours in the day? If any man walk in the day, he stumbleth not, because he seeth the light of this world. But if a man walk in the night, he stumbleth, because there is no light in him. These things said he: and after that he saith unto them, Our friend Lazarus sleepeth; but I go, that I may awake him out of sleep. Then said his disciples, Lord, if he sleep, he shall do well. Howbeit Jesus spake of his death: but they thought that he had spoken of taking of rest in sleep. Then said Jesus unto them plainly, Lazarus is dead. And I am glad for your sakes that I was not there, to the intent ye may believe; nevertheless let us go unto him. Then said Thomas, which is called Didymus, unto his fellowdisciples, Let us also go, that we may die with him. Then when Jesus came, he found that he had lain in the grave four days already. Now Bethany was nigh unto Jerusalem, about fifteen furlongs off: and many of the Jews came to Martha and Mary, to comfort them concerning their brother. Then Martha, as soon as she heard that Jesus was coming, went and met him: but Mary sat still in the house. Then said Martha unto Jesus, Lord, if thou hadst been here, my brother had not died. But I know, that even now, whatsoever thou wilt ask of God, God will give it thee. Jesus saith unto her, Thy brother shall rise again. Martha saith unto him, I know that he shall rise again in the resurrection at the last day. Jesus said unto her, I am the resurrection, and the life: he that believeth in me, though he were dead, yet shall he live: and whosoever liveth and believeth in me shall never die. Believest thou this? She saith unto him, Yea, Lord: I believe that thou art the Christ, the Son of God, which should come into the world. And when she had so said, she went her way, and called Mary her sister secretly, saying, The Master is come, and calleth for thee. As soon as she heard that, she arose quickly, and came unto him. Now Jesus was not yet come into the town, but was in that place where Martha met him. The Jews then which were with her in the house, and comforted her, when they saw Mary, that she rose up hastily and went out, followed her, saying, She goeth unto the grave to weep there. Then when Mary was come where Jesus was, and saw him, she fell down at his feet, saying unto him, Lord, if thou hadst been here, my brother had not died. When Jesus therefore saw her weeping, and the Jews also weeping which came with her, he groaned in the spirit, and was troubled, and said, Where have ye laid him? They said unto him, Lord, come and see. Jesus wept. Then said the Jews, Behold how he loved him! And some of them said, Could not this man, which opened the eyes of the blind, have caused that even this man should not have died? Jesus therefore again groaning in himself cometh to the grave. It was a cave, and a stone lay upon it. Jesus said, Take ye away the stone. Martha, the sister of him that was dead, saith unto him, Lord, by this time he stinketh: for he hath been dead four days. Jesus saith unto her, Said I not unto thee, that, if thou wouldest believe, thou shouldest see the glory of God? Then they took away the stone from the place where the dead was laid. And Jesus lifted up his eyes, and said, Father, I thank thee that thou hast heard me. And I knew that thou hearest me always: but because of the people which stand by I said it, that they may believe that thou hast sent me. And when he thus had spoken, he cried with a loud voice, Lazarus, come forth. And he that was dead came forth, bound hand and foot with graveclothes: and his face was bound about with a napkin. Jesus saith unto them, Loose him, and let him go. Then many of the Jews which came to Mary, and had seen the things which Jesus did, believed on him. (John 11:1–45)

And I saw a new heaven and a new earth: for the first heaven and the first earth were passed away; and there was no more sea. And I John saw the holy city, new Jerusalem, coming down from God out of heaven, prepared as a bride adorned for her husband. And I heard a great voice out of heaven saying, Behold, the tabernacle of God is with men, and he will dwell with them, and they shall be his people, and God himself shall be with them, and be their God. And God shall wipe away all tears from their eyes; and there shall be no more death, neither sorrow, nor crying, neither shall there be any more pain: for the former things are passed away. And he that sat upon the throne said, Behold, I make all things new. And he said unto me, Write: for these words are true and faithful. (Rev. 21:1–5)

And he shewed me a pure river of water of life, clear as crystal, proceeding out of the throne of God and of the Lamb. In the midst of the street of it, and on either side of the river, was there the tree of life, which bare twelve manner of fruits, and yielded her fruit every month: and the leaves of the tree were for the healing of the nations. And there shall be no more curse: but the throne of God and of the Lamb shall be in it; and his servants shall serve him: and they shall see his face; and his name shall be in their foreheads. And there shall be no night there; and they need no candle, neither light of the sun; for the Lord God giveth them light: and they shall reign for ever and ever. And he said unto me, These sayings are faithful and true: and the Lord God of the holy prophets sent his angel to shew unto his servants the things which must shortly be done. (Rev. 22:1–6)

There was a man of the Pharisees, named Nicodemus, a ruler of the Jews: the same came to Jesus by night, and said unto him, Rabbi, we know that thou art a teacher come from God: for no man can do these miracles that thou doest, except God be with him. Jesus answered and said unto him, Verily, verily, I say unto thee, Except a man be born again, he cannot see the kingdom of God. Nicodemus saith unto him, How can a man be born when he is old? can he enter the second time into his mother's womb, and be born? Jesus answered, Verily, verily, I say unto thee, Except a man be born of water and of the Spirit, he cannot enter into the kingdom of God. That which is born of the flesh is flesh; and that which is born of the Spirit is spirit. Marvel not that I said unto thee, Ye must be born again. The wind bloweth where it listeth, and thou hearest the sound thereof, but canst not tell whence it cometh, and whither it goeth: so is every one that is born of the Spirit. Nicodemus answered and said unto him, How can these things be? Jesus answered and said unto him, Art thou a master of Israel, and knowest not these things? Verily, verily, I say unto thee, We speak that we do know, and testify that we have seen; and ye receive not our witness. If I have told you earthly things, and ye believe not, how shall ye believe, if I tell you of heavenly things? And no man hath ascended up to heaven, but he that came down from heaven, even the Son of man which is in heaven. And as Moses lifted up the serpent in the wilderness, even so must the Son of man be lifted up: that whosoever believeth in him should not perish, but have eternal life. For God so loved the world, that he gave his only begotten Son, that whosoever believeth in him should not perish, but have everlasting life. For God sent not his Son into the world to condemn the world; but that the world through him might be saved. He that believeth on him is not condemned: but he that believeth not is condemned already, because he hath not believed in the name of the only begotten Son of God. (John 3:1–18)

Verily, verily, I say unto you, He that entereth not by the door into the sheepfold, but climbeth up some other way, the same is a thief and a robber. But he that entereth in by the door is the shepherd of the sheep. To him the porter openeth; and the sheep hear his voice: and he calleth his own sheep by name, and leadeth them out. And when he putteth forth his own sheep, he goeth before them, and the sheep follow him: for they know his voice. And a stranger will they not follow, but will flee from him: for they know not the voice of strangers. This parable spake Jesus unto them: but they understood not what things they were which he spake unto them. Then said Jesus unto them again, Verily, verily, I say unto you, I am the door of the sheep. All that ever came before me are thieves and robbers: but the sheep did not hear them. I am the door: by me if any man enter in, he shall be saved, and shall go in and out, and find pasture. The thief cometh not, but for to steal, and to kill, and to destroy: I am come that they might have life, and that they might have it more abundantly. I am the good shepherd: the good shepherd giveth his life for the sheep. But he that is an hireling, and not the shepherd, whose own the sheep are not, seeth the wolf coming, and leaveth the sheep, and fleeth: and the wolf catcheth them, and scattereth the sheep. The hireling fleeth, because he is an hireling, and careth not for the sheep. I am the good shepherd, and know my sheep, and am known of mine. As the Father knoweth me, even so know I the Father: and I lay down my life for the sheep. And other sheep I have, which are not of this fold: them also I must bring, and they shall hear my voice; and there shall be one fold, and one shepherd. Therefore doth my Father love me, because I lay down my life, that I might take it again. No man taketh it from me, but I lay it down of myself. I have power to lay it down, and I have power to take it again. This commandment have I received of my Father. There was a division therefore again among the Jews for these sayings. And many of them said, He hath a devil, and is mad; why hear ye him? Others said, These are not the words of him that hath a devil. Can a devil open the eyes of the blind? And it was at Jerusalem the feast of the dedication, and it was winter. And Jesus walked in the temple in Solomon's porch. Then came the Jews round about him, and said unto him, How long dost thou make us to doubt? If thou be the Christ, tell us plainly. Jesus answered them, I told you, and ye believed not: the works that I do in my Father's name, they bear witness of me. But ye believe not, because ye are not of my sheep, as I said unto you. My sheep hear my voice, and I know them, and they follow me: and I give unto them eternal life; and they shall never perish, neither shall any man pluck them out of my hand. My Father, which gave them me, is greater than all; and no man is able to pluck them out of my Father's hand. I and my Father are one. (John 10:1–30)

Let not your heart be troubled: ye believe in God, believe also in me. In my Father's house are many mansions: if it were not so, I would have told you. I go to prepare a place for you. And if I go and prepare a place for you, I will come again, and receive you unto myself; that where I am, there ye may be also. And whither I go ye know, and the way ye know. Thomas saith unto him, Lord, we know not whither thou goest; and how can we know the way? Jesus saith unto him, I am the way, the truth, and the life: no man cometh unto the Father, but by me. (John 14:1–6)

Then the same day at evening, being the first day of the week, when the doors were shut where the disciples were assembled for fear of the Jews, came Jesus and stood in the midst, and saith unto them, Peace be unto you. And when he had so said, he shewed unto them his hands and his side. Then were the disciples glad, when they saw the Lord. Then said Jesus to them again, Peace be unto you: as my Father hath sent me, even so send I you. And when he had said this, he breathed on them, and saith unto them, Receive ye the Holy Ghost: whose soever sins ye remit, they are remitted unto them; and whose soever sins ye retain, they are retained. But Thomas, one of the twelve, called Didymus, was not with them when Jesus came. The other disciples therefore said unto him, We have seen the Lord. But he said unto them, Except I shall see in his hands the print of the nails, and put my finger into the print of the nails, and thrust my hand into his side, I will not believe. And after eight days again his disciples were within, and Thomas with them: then came Jesus, the doors being shut, and stood in the midst, and said, Peace be unto you. Then saith he to Thomas, Reach hither thy finger, and behold my hands; and reach hither thy hand, and thrust it into my side: and be not faithless, but believing. And Thomas answered and said unto him, My Lord and my God. Jesus saith unto him, Thomas, because thou hast seen me, thou hast believed: blessed are they that have not seen, and yet have believed. And many other signs truly did Jesus in the presence of his disciples, which are not written in this book: but these are written, that ye might believe that Jesus is the Christ, the Son of God; and that believing ye might have life through his name. (John 20:19–31)

CPSIA information can be obtained at www.ICGtesting.com
Printed in the USA
BVOW03s0923270514

354408BV00001B/4/P

9 781490 802893